THE GEISHA SECRET

ANCIENT DATING RITUALS PROVEN TO WIN A MODERN MAN'S HEART

HANAKO

FassFrankfurt Publishers

THE GEISHA SECRET

FassFrankfurt Media, LLC
FassFrankfurt Publishers
802 Sixth Avenue, Suite 200
New York, NY 10001

Book design by Sea Leaf Publications

Printed in the United States of America
2nd Edition

ISBN: 978-0-9835777-2-0

To all the women who hope to find love

Contents

ABOUT THE AUTHOR

The Geisha Secret was written by a dating and relationship expert, under the pen name Hanako. Recognizing that the geisha has fascinated men for centuries, Hanako extensively studied the geisha as a means of understanding the secret of attracting men. Little has been written about the true geisha. Most westerners are familiar with the fictional geisha as depicted in western novels and movies. The true geisha lived in the secretive and exclusive flower and willow world. Outsiders were not allowed entry into her world and it was taboo to reveal details about the geisha's life. Hanako brings together the geisha's history, revealing how the geisha captured men's hearts. She applies the ways of the geisha to today's modern world so that you know the secret to winning a man's heart.

The name Hanako is Japanese for flower *(hana)* child *(ko)*, which is symbolic of the flower and willow world. Hanako represents all of the women who are hoping to find a man or to be married – a flower bud ready to be nurtured so she can blossom into an exquisite bloom that is desired and loved by men. Hanako is the guide who will teach you *The Geisha Secret* and how to forever change the way men perceive you. She has passed *The Geisha Secret* on to you so that if carefully followed, then it will change your life as it has done for so many other women.

THE GEISHA MYSTIQUE

Behind the Japanese geisha's strikingly painted face, exquisite silk kimono, and flawlessly choreographed dance, lies *The Geisha Secret* – the definitive way for women to prepare for finding love. The geisha practiced her secrets for centuries, captivating men with her beauty, intellect, and masterful talents. Contrary to the American depiction of geisha as high-end courtesans, geisha were artists – an exclusive class of accomplished dancers, musicians, and conversationalists, performing at the highest levels of Japanese society.[1] Men respected, revered, and admired the geisha. They longed to know her and the mysteries of the flower and willow world, the world where the geisha lived and few were allowed entry. Access to the geisha was limited and it was her exclusiveness that made men desire her more. Men passionately loved her as she uncovered men's deepest desires, leaving her image of gracefulness and beauty forever imprinted on history.

Today, the geisha is more relevant than ever because modern women have lost their touch with men. *The Geisha Secret* will lead you through a journey of transformation, from an ordinary woman into a woman who is loved and desired by men. You will learn how to accentuate your strongest attributes and become the best woman you can be. You will be exposed to the geisha's way of life, learning how to achieve success with men. *The Geisha Secret* will show you how to embrace your femininity and captivate a man, while remaining an independent woman. It will teach you that you should never lose your identity to gain a man's love. A woman is more attractive when she has her own ideas and pursuits, while retaining the sensitivity and ability to understand and respect a man's needs. You will discover that if you possess insight into a man's desires, coupled with unique talents and achievements that define you, as well as the kindness and beauty that lies within you, then a man will love you more than any other woman.

The geisha mastered the art of desirability and men were drawn to her because she was man's ideal female companion. Over the past century, women's role in society has changed, but men have remained the same. They continue in pursuit of the ideal female companion. They desire a woman who is feminine, beautiful, and skilled at understanding a man and his needs, while also being accomplished and independent, without being contentious. They want a woman who has mastered the delicate balance between being supportive and attentive in one moment and being decisive and independent in another.

The Geisha Secret is what every modern woman must know if she wants a boyfriend or to be married. When you follow and faithfully practice *The Rituals* of *The Geisha Secret*, your relationships with men will change. Men will admire your inner and outer beauty. They will want to hear what you have to say, desire to be near you, and want you to love them as much as they love you. I invite you to uncover the mystique and allure of the geisha, where you will learn *The Geisha Secret* and the way to win a man's heart.

Everyone wants to know how magic is created. The geisha world has such deep secrets and techniques – I could spend my whole life trying to find its core. After three or four hundred years of history, its secrets are still intact – and always will be.[2]

THE RITUALS

The Rituals describe the ancient techniques of the geisha, recounting her history and how she became one of the most desired women in the world. The geisha possessed distinct qualities and talents that have been perfected so that she could be her best: from making herself uniquely beautiful and accentuating her attributes to emphasizing her femininity and becoming a subtle vision of sensuality. Her beauty was deep and vast, and her words and presence were healing and uplifting. To be in her presence was to experience a fantasy – a world of exquisite beauty where men indulged in the finest cuisine and were privy to the best in art and conversation. The geisha was, first and foremost, an artist, exhibiting great talent as a musician and dancer. Her art included writing calligraphy and performing the intricate tea ceremony. To be one of the few who knew her, meant that you were a friend of a renowned artist. As the geisha had a clear vision of how to perfect her talents, *The Rituals* will help you determine what is your art as a woman. When you uncover your art, you will possess the ability to understand your best qualities and talents and exemplify them.

For you to become admired and desired as the geisha was, you must practice *The Rituals* with dedication and perfection, with your heart at the soul of each *Ritual*. *The Rituals* are not a quick fix for problems with dating or relationships. Instead, they are a way of life that will help you become forever desirable to men and empower you to be the best woman you can be. Each *Ritual* can be practiced independently, but they are most effective when they are implemented together. When you allow *The Rituals* to become the essence of your being, you will be transformed into the ideal female companion. Men will be intrigued by you, love you, and seek to give you their hearts with the hope of their affection being returned. Appreciate and practice *The Rituals* as they will help you develop a renewed sense of self and bring you success with love.

Ritual 1   Make Yourself Uniquely Beautiful

Ritual 2   Embrace Your Femininity

Ritual 3   Demonstrate Subtle Sex Appeal

Ritual 4   Embody Elegance

Ritual 5   Exhibit Intelligence and Accomplishment

Ritual 6   Exercise Humility in Everything You Do

Ritual 7   Act with Kindness

Ritual 8   Perform Thoughtful Acts

Ritual 9   Be the Prize that is Pursued

Ritual 10   Wait to Give Yourself to a Man

Ritual 11   Be at Ease in All of Your Endeavors

Ritual 12   Show Your Appreciation

Ritual 13   Be Compassionate

Ritual 14   Be Deliberate in Your Communication

Ritual 15   Be Attentive at Key Moments

Ritual 16   Deeply Connect to a Man

Ritual 17   Allow a Man to Embrace his Maleness

Ritual 18   Be an Independent Woman

Ritual 19   Be a Dynamic Hostess

Ritual 20 Keep a Man Intrigued

The geisha created a life of beauty. She made herself into the image of the perfect woman, the embodiment of Japanese culture and refinement, a living work of art.[1]

MAKE YOURSELF UNIQUELY BEAUTIFUL

Beauty

The geisha transformed herself into an iconic beauty

A man fortunate enough to be in the presence of the geisha was immediately mesmerized by her beauty. Her makeup was meticulously applied, accentuating her lips to create a perfect rosebud against her delicately painted white face. This enabled her to stand out when performing on a dimly lit stage. Her luxurious black hair was ornately styled and worn up, revealing the nape of her neck. She adorned herself with accessories – parasols, fans and handbags – crafted from handmade paper, silk, and bamboo. There were many aspects that were integral to the geisha's appearance, but her kimonos were the most critical.

The geisha valued her kimonos over all other possessions and referred to them as her *soul* and the indispensable badge of her craft.¹ She wore the most exquisite kimonos in all of Japan – equivalent to today's finest couture dresses, costing a year's salary or more for each of them. Being one-of-a-kind works of art, the geisha took an active role in designing her kimonos. She chose the colors and patterns, which revealed her sense of style and personality. The design of her kimono symbolized her status within her *hanamachi*.² The *hanamachi* were the flower towns within the flower and willow world, also known as the *karyukai*. Throughout the *karyukai* in Japan, geisha belonged to different *hanamachi*. The most famous *hanamachi* is Gion in the city of Kyoto. The most beautiful, talented, and accomplished geisha came from Gion. A geisha from Gion started her training as a *maiko* (apprentice geisha). When she completed the arduous process of becoming a full-fledged geisha, she graduated to *geiko*.

The style of the geisha's kimono was important as it exhibited her current title. For the *maiko*, her kimono emphasized her youth and beauty. Her wide sleeves indicated that she was unmarried, and fluttering her sleeves was a declaration of love. A junior *maiko* wore kimonos richly patterned with chrysanthemums, water patterns, maple leaves, autumn grasses, turtles and cranes, and other symbols, reflecting the season. A senior *maiko* wore kimonos with fewer patterns and with one shoulder undecorated, while a *geiko* wore kimonos without any patterns above the *obi* (sash). The designs on the kimono and the geisha's accessories alternated according to the season, reflecting the natural elements of each season.

The geisha's kimono was twice the size of a standard kimono worn by Japanese women. Made of a single piece of *tan* (cloth), dressing in a kimono was a difficult skill that had to be learned. Many geisha had assistant dressers to help them dress. A kimono did not have any buttons or fasteners and was wrapped around the geisha, tucked together with the left side over right and seared in the front with a dozen braids.

The kimono was completed with the tying of the *obi* around the waist, the hardest part of dressing the geisha because it required strength and dexterity. Having a good assistant dresser was critical for the geisha's success.[3] As an artist who performed at a professional level, the geisha believed that no matter how accomplished she was, her hard work was to no avail if she did not have the proper clothes to compliment her beauty and accomplishments.[4] Guests of the *karyukai* appreciated and admired the geisha's appearance as much as her artistic accomplishments. The *maiko*, as an apprentice geisha, wore the most elaborate and complicated costume, turning her into a work of art. Accentuating the geisha's beauty was most important at the *maiko* stage because she was first being introduced as a geisha and guests knew very little about her. The art contained in her dress was symbolic of the artist she was to become as a *geiko*. When she graduated to a *geiko*, she had reached the level of an established artist and became well known within the *hanamachi*. Her dress and make-up remained exquisite, yet less elaborate. Accentuating your physical beauty is most important as the first time you meet a man is equivalent to being first introduced. As the *maiko* made a profound impression on men with her unique, exquisite beauty, you should be memorable to a man when he first lays eyes on you.

Exemplify beauty and men will be drawn to you

Every woman has it within herself to be beautiful, no matter her shape or size. It is up to you to bring forth both your best inner and outer qualities so that you shine on the outside and men take notice of you. A man is initially attracted to what he first sees. Yet, each man has his own preference, which makes all shapes and sizes beautiful. What differentiates women from one another and elicits an immediate response from men as it relates specifically to their appearance is irrelevant to a woman's shape or size. Stripped down to her base features, the woman who stands out may not be naturally the most beautiful woman, but she stands out as unique because she understands how to make herself more beautiful. She wears her clothes to accentuate her feminine figure, yet done tastefully to enhance her physical beauty. Her physique is toned and healthy, with skin that radiates. She is energized and confident and knows how to make herself more attractive. Every woman has it within her to be the woman men notice first.

The process begins with accentuating and tending to your appearance so that you look your best. As you are working to bring out your best physical traits, remember that equally as important to your exterior beauty is your inner beauty. In most cases, your inner and outer beauty in combination is what will entice a man to ask you on a second date and desire to date you long-term. Your physical beauty should merely be a window into the abundance of your inner beauty. Significant time should be spent developing your inner beauty – possessing qualities such as kindness and compassion, and being accomplished. Realize the significance of your outer beauty, however your inner beauty is what is most attractive. It is difficult for a man to know how deep your beauty runs without giving him an indication of your interpersonal qualities. Tend to your physical beauty and devote attention to it as the geisha did because a man is more likely to notice you if you look your best. You will further draw him in when he discovers that your beauty is deep and vast, unlike any other.

Achieve exceptional beauty

To feel and look your best, there are practices that will enhance your beauty that are easy to remember and to incorporate into daily life. Many of them you are already aware of, but know that if you incorporate all of them as one, then you your beauty will stand out to men. In combination they will build your confidence and instill a positive mindset. When you walk into a room, you will embody a presence that men will notice. To become the woman who stands out among all others, begin with honestly assessing yourself and decide which areas in your life-style should be changed or improved. Do you feel that your hair rarely looks nice? Are you frustrated because you are not eating as healthy as you should, resulting in feeling sluggish and bloated? Is exercise your greatest struggle because you feel as if you never have time for it? Begin enhancing your beauty by incorporating a little change into your life every single day. As the geisha devoted much time to transforming herself into a vision of beauty, you should be able to do the same with a commitment to making some small changes. Your transformation will take some time if you want it to be long lasting. Tend to your body and provide yourself the best you can to ensure your own health and well-being. View accentuating your physical beauty as a healthy way of life that will bring an abundance of positive energy to your body, soul, and mind.

❋ **Nourish your body with healthy food**
What you put into your body directly reflects your appearance and your energy level. Own your body and your health. Try to eat food in its most pure state, which will cut down on unnecessary calories. This will enable your body to be filled with the nutrients it needs to help enhance your beauty. Practice moderation when eating unhealthy foods, and avoid processed foods. Food is processed to enhance flavor and extend shelf life, which is done by using unnatural products. When you eat most packaged food, you are filling your body with chemicals that it is not meant to have.

Consuming too many processed foods will effect your appearance and your internal body over the long-term. Along with eliminating processed foods, limit your intake of sugar. Many products that advertise low fat, fat free, or low calorie are misleading because they are high in sugar. For sweets, decide how many days a week you can eat them and commit to it – maybe only on the weekends or three times a week. Choose fruit as an alternative for dessert. Also, consume fatty foods in moderation. Do not substitute low-fat, processed foods for the fatty foods. Stick to low-fat, natural food (e.g., fresh fruits and vegetables, natural grains, fresh fish, and grain-raised organic chicken). There are many healthy foods that taste great and will make you feel better. Seek them out and incorporate them as the staple of your daily diet. By eliminating processed foods and limiting yourself to a small amount of sugar and fat, your skin will glow and your body will slim down to its natural size.

❋ **Give to your body rather than deprive it**
Never starve yourself or deprive yourself of important nutrients to lose weight. The media uses celebrities and models as the definition of beauty, but that does not mean that that is the best way to look or what women should be striving towards. A skinny woman whose primary focus in life is to stay thin and who believes that her skeletal frame is what makes her beautiful, is nothing more than a skinny woman in a shell. The majority of men prefer a woman whose body is defined with curves. Comparing yourself to other women will only cause frustration. Accept your natural body and embrace it. Focus on how to make your body look its best for your size and frame by maintaining an ideal

weight through eating healthy and exercising regularly. Remember that there are many aspects that make you beautiful – it is not your body alone.

❋ **Exercise to tone your body and feel your best**
Exercise is a necessity for your body, mind, and spirit. You may feel that you can never be the woman who exercises constantly, but do not look at exercise as a dreaded chore. Walking to a location rather than driving is exercise. Taking a stroll in the park with a friend is also exercise. There are other forms of exercise that you can do that require greater exertion, such as yoga, running, soccer, tennis, or pilates, which are great for the body. Exercise does not have to be expensive. If you do not live near a gym or cannot spend the money on a health club or gym membership, then you can run, cycle, or swim. Alternatively, there are many exercise DVDs that you can buy and do at home. Your physique will improve if you exercise for forty-five minutes for four days a week, which is not much time each week. Write down a weekly routine to help you stay focused and follow through with it. For instance, you can play tennis on one day of the week, go to yoga on another day of the week, and take long walks on two other days of the week. Choose a routine that produces results and is most enjoyable for you so that you are able to maintain the regime over the long-term. Also, take advantage of opportunities to walk instead of drive. If you do not live far from your work, then walk to and from rather than drive or take public transportation. Use the stairs instead of an elevator. Perhaps at work, try walking during lunchtime. An extra ten minutes of walking here and there adds up over a week. You will find that continuous physical activity will not only

help you look your best, but you will also feel better mentally and physically. Men will find you more attractive because of the positive energy that you gain from exercise.

- **Rejuvenate with sleep and vitamins**
  Sleep is critical to rejuvenating your body so that you have energy and look and feel refreshed. Adequate sleep also helps in preventing wrinkles and pre-mature aging. The more sleep you get, the better you will look and feel. If you feel tired, then you will look tired. If you feel refreshed, then you will look refreshed. Vitamins will also help to give your body energy. They assist with fighting off illness and nourish your body with any nutrient deficiency you may be experiencing. Taking vitamins and getting enough sleep are easy ways to keep your body healthy.

- **Live healthy**
  Limit your intake of alcohol and do not smoke. This includes being a social smoker. When you smoke, you fill your body with toxins. The more you smoke, the faster your body ages. Plus, most men find smoking unattractive. Smoking will make your clothes and breath smell bad. When consuming alcohol, you should limit it. Alcohol is often loaded with calories and sugar. Drinking a lot of it is counter-productive to all of the work that you do to maintain a healthy life.

- **Tend to your skin, especially your face**
  A man spends most of his time looking at your face. Your skin should look the best that it can. There are many men who feel a woman's body is second to her face and that a beautiful face is the most important

physical feature of a woman. If you can afford it, then try to get facials regularly. If facials are too costly, then come up with a regime to clean your skin with quality products. It is important to avoid sunbathing for long periods of time. A little sun is healthy, but sunbathe too much and you could be accelerating the aging process. You cannot reverse the effects of too much sun. The only remedy is prevention. The better you take care of your skin, the slower you will age and the prettier your face will be as you grow older. Since the body will change over time, then men look more at facial characteristics when searching for a long-term mate.

❊ Dress well to accentuate your beauty and flatter your body

When a woman dresses well, she is twice as beautiful. Make the extra effort to dress well. This does not mean that you have to buy an expensive wardrobe. Realize that men do not care that your clothes are expensive or that you are wearing the latest fashion. When you dress to follow fashion trends, you are dressing for other women, not men. When you dress for men, you should wear clothes that accent your best physical assets, whether your clothes are ten years old, purchased on sale, or are of the latest fashion. If you are at a loss on how to dress, then ask a friend with good taste to give you tips. The key is to wear clothes that enhance your assets. If you have great legs, wear skirts. If you have great arms, wear sleeveless shirts. Practice the rules of simple beauty. Your makeup should be natural so that you look beautiful, as if you are not wearing any makeup at all. Your clothing should enhance the silhouette of your body, but not reveal so much to appear naked. The sight of you should tempt a man to imagine.

❋ Develop your own sense of style
The geisha had a style that was uniquely hers, making her more memorable to a man. Having your own style exhibits feminine strength and beauty. Your own style distinguishes you from the masses and shows that you are willing to take a risk. It also shows that it is important for you to be yourself. These are all qualities that men find attractive. By expressing confidence and a strong sense of self through your appearance, you are enhancing your beauty. The geisha created a beauty and world that uniquely belonged to her, leaving her imprint on the world. Your beauty should be forever memorable to a man so that it brings out the best of you.

A woman should own her beauty

You possess the ability to accentuate your beauty so that you look your best. The same held true for Christy and Laurie, best friends living in New York City while in their early thirties. Both were working hard and trying to meet men. Both had similar features and bodies, but each took a different approach as to how they tended to their bodies. Each had the chance to improve their future with men by looking their best. Yet, only one actively worked to do so, resulting in her being more successful with men.

Christy was perfect on paper with an undergraduate degree and MBA from Ivy League universities, followed by a highly coveted, powerful job on Wall Street. She was a bi-lingual world traveler and very successful. She even owned an apartment in Manhattan and a house in the Hamptons, a rarity for a woman in her thirties. She was also well educated on business and current affairs. It was amazing to watch her converse with men, many who were leaders in their industries. Men liked being around Christy, as did women, and everyone was sure to invite her to social events. Between work and friends, Christy was never short of invitations to parties and dinners. However, the one thing she wanted most – a date – rarely happened.

When Christy graduated from business school, the men she liked would only ask her out on dates every now and then. Christy struggled with her weight and never exercised, which effected her mental well-being and self-confidence with men. At this point in her life, Christy was moderately over her ideal weight and was visibly upset that she did not have a boyfriend. As time passed, Christy put on more weight each year and became more depressed about men, resulting in less dates. Eventually, men who were equally successful and intelligent as she rarely asked her out. Friends found it difficult to set her up. Christy wasn't lacking in personality. She had an incredible career and could have supported a husband and a family. The problem was that men of the caliber she wanted were not attracted to her physically, coupled with her low self-confidence when viewing herself as a woman that men want to date. Christy had numerous male friends, more than most women do. They respected her greatly, but none of them transitioned into a boyfriend. Yet, there were changes Christy could make in her life to be the woman men desire. Christy already had many qualities men seek in a lifelong partner – intelligence, accomplishment, humility, and an easygoing, light demeanor.

When Christy graduated from business school, all that she had to do to improve her self-confidence and physique was to establish an exercise routine and eat healthier. She needed to lose some weight and tone her body to put her in an improved state both physically and mentally – a predicament many women face, which is achievable if they commit to becoming healthy. Christy's challenge was that food was always a big part of her life. She was an excellent cook and her life revolved around excessive meals with no dedication to exercise. Should Christy decide to work towards getting to a healthy weight and tending to her body, she will then look her best. Men that she likes will be interested in her. Every woman should have options and have the opportunity to attract the man who is right for her.

Christy's friend, Laurie, was in a similar situation as Christy after business school. Laurie was not as quite successful as Christy in respect to her job and social life. However, Laurie embarked on a different path. Initially, like Christy, Laurie also ate excessively and rarely exercised. She would snack on sweets throughout the day and never count calories. If she was sitting with a friend who was eating donuts, then she would eat three of them. After two years of these eating habits, Laurie could not ignore the fact that she had put on over twenty pounds and her clothes no longer fit. She had lost her drive to socialize and spent less time going out. Much to her dismay, she was also going on a lot less dates and was depressed about men. Ignoring her problem, she bought a new wardrobe for her new body and continued on with her same eating habits, exercising rarely, and putting on more weight, while spending her time alone or with her closest girlfriends. One day, her parents said that she had to get healthy or her life would lead to a path of problems. Laurie was very close to her parents and their comments hit her hard. Rather than shying away from her predicament, Laurie started talking openly to her friends and family. She asked for their advice and input on how she could get back to a healthy life style.

To begin, Laurie committed to following a strict diet and exercise routine. Everyone quickly noticed a difference. Within months, her body had completely transformed. Laurie looked great. She started introducing some of the 'bad' foods back into her diet, but she did not eat them excessively like she had in the past. She was fine with one piece of cake whereas before she would have had a second slice. Her body had trained itself to be satisfied with less sugar and less food. What was even more amazing was that Laurie was not starving herself nor denying herself all of the pleasures that food offers. She continued to tone and slim down because she was exercising regularly. She had rediscovered her love for sports and was actively playing in leagues.

By no means was Laurie at an unhealthy weight, like many models. Laurie was a healthy weight for her size with a toned body and men took notice because she looked and felt great. When Laurie would walk down the street in a form-fitting dress and high heels, she would catch men's eyes. When she would go to a bar, men would ask her out. Friends were setting her up again. Laurie was now at the point where she was turning down eligible men who did not interest her.

Laurie's life had taken a different path from Christy's because Laurie made the effort to be healthy and look her best. Laurie continues to exercise and maintain a balanced diet. She also dresses well and tends to her body by getting facials, manicures, and pedicures. If one looks at Laurie, then one instantly sees a pretty and well-put together woman. Although Laurie does not have as dynamic of a personality and is not as intelligent or successful as Christy, this does not initially matter because men were first attracted to Laurie's physical appearance. Men are visual and initially gravitate towards what they see in front of them. A woman's inner beauty will make her more beautiful and desirable in the long-term, but it is difficult for a man to discover a woman's inner beauty if he has little or no physical draw to a woman upon first meeting her. The geisha understood this concept and devoted much time to her appearance. Her beauty stopped men in their tracks and fascinated men for centuries.

Be uniquely beautiful – practice *Ritual 1.*

The geisha put much effort into her appearance and was universally recognized for her striking, exquisite beauty. She understood how a woman's physical beauty can increase a man's desire and attraction to a woman, enticing him to want to know more about her. You have the ability to accentuate your features so that you are more attractive to men. As you work to look your best, remember that the geisha did not define her physical beauty by the size of her body. Instead, her beauty was defined by her striking face, dark smooth hair, exquisite kimono draped across her figure, elegant walk, and delicate touch. It is the presence that you exude, coupled with tending to your body and appearance that will make men notice you.

She (the maiko) has the classic looks of a Heian princess, as though she might have stepped out of an eleventh-century scroll painting. Her face is a perfect oval. Her skin is white and flawless, her hair black as a raven's wing. Her brows are half moons, her mouth a delicate rosebud. Her neck is long and sensuous, her figure gently rounded.[5]

EMBRACE YOUR FEMININITY

Feminine

The geisha valued the power of her femininity

The geisha understood the power of her feminine mystique and she accentuated these attributes to influence men. Taking the Japanese fashion of the time and elaborating upon it, the geisha created a style that was more feminine than the traditional Japanese dress. This was prominently displayed in the *maiko* costume of an apprentice geisha. The popular image of the geisha adorned in a sumptuous kimono, accented with white makeup and elaborate hair ornaments, is the dress of the *maiko*. A *maiko* developed her craft as an artist and worked towards earning the title of *geiko*. When she became a *geiko*, her kimono changed to being more subdued and she only painted her face white when performing. Whereas a *maiko's* dress was precisely designed to accentuate her appearance because as she was still learning how to be as skilled and accomplished as a full-fledged *geiko*, it was believed her most attractive attributes to men were her beauty and femininity. Beauty is seen as innate while artistry is learned. It took many years of practice before the geisha reached the level of a professional artist. When she achieved the title of *geiko*, her great artistic talent transcended her beauty to a higher level few women achieved.

To begin her journey to become a *geiko*, a young woman aspiring to become a geisha moved into an *okiya* (a house where geisha lived and trained) as a *shikomi* (the first stage as an apprentice geisha). She started at the bottom of a strict hierarchy and earned her place with humbling duties. She scrubbed floors and performed other cleaning duties, but also did so looking tidy. She began learning how to dance and play the *shamisen* (a three-stringed instrument), percussion, and flute. Her goal was to acclimate to the traditional *hanamachi* life. [1] She completed her *shikomi* training with a formal dance test at the *kaburenjo* (dance institute), graded by prominent *hanamachi* grandees. If she passed, then she was ready to become a fledgling *maiko* or a *minarai* (meaning looking and learning). Throughout her career, the geisha continued to observe and study, training for many years, so that she could master her art. It was this steady devotion to her art that developed her character and made her stand out as one of the most accomplished women in Japan.

When a geisha completed the *minarai* stage, she formally debuted as a *maiko*. She was ready to wear the elaborate, feminine dress designed to awe the onlooker. Every detail of the *maiko's* appearance was calculated to emphasize her femininity and seductiveness. Her jet-black hair was worn in the dramatic *wareshinobu* style (a round curve on the top and sides with a round bun in the middle), wrapped around a red silk ribbon, adorned with approximately a dozen various combs, flutters, hairpins, and silk bands that related to the month and season. Her face was painted with a white mask called a *shironuri*, creating an electrifying effect in contrast to her delicate dress and symbolizing that she now belonged to the flower and willow world. Her white mask was softened with hints of blush on her cheeks and around her eyes. Her eyes were rimmed with purple eyeliner, smudged slightly at the corners to emphasize their perfect almond shape. Her eyebrows were shaved and penciled in a similar shade to create *ryubi* (willow brows). Only her lower lip was painted with crimson lipstick to create a tiny rosebud, while her upper lip was left white, blending with the rest of her face. Her upper chest and most of her shoulders were also painted white, leaving a sharp *W* shape of bare skin leading down the nape of her neck.[2] Men have described a *maiko* in full costume as the Japanese ideal of feminine beauty.[3]

As the geisha valued her femininity, you should understand how your own femininity influences men. The *maiko* was transformed into a vision of femininity by how she dressed, the style she wore her make-up and hair, and the way in which she spoke and moved. Every day you have the opportunity to present yourself in a feminine manner. By accentuating your feminine attributes, you are reminding a man that you are a woman. One of the most powerful attributes you possess as a woman is that you are in fact a woman. Celebrate and cherish your femininity. By mastering the art of femininity, you can invoke this age-old powerful tool to attract the man of your dreams.

Personify femininity and embrace being a female

If you understand how to be feminine and its influence in the presence of men, then you will possess the ability to draw a man's attention. It is your feminine qualities that will make him desire you. A man does not want to be with a woman who has similar traits to a female warrior. For many women, to achieve independence and accomplishment they have mimicked men in all aspects of their lives. They have taken on masculine traits, which they incorrectly believed that they needed to do so. In the process, they lost sight of their true self as a woman. It is a woman's feminine mystique that has attracted men since the beginning of mankind. A woman should always retain her femininity. A woman can be professionally accomplished, while being feminine at the same time. In fact, these two qualities in combination (independence and femininity) will make you more interesting and attractive. This is at the heart of why men were enamored with the geisha. A man is deeply attracted to an independent, confident woman who balances her strength with a feminine touch.

The geisha was years ahead of her contemporaries and resembles today's modern woman as she was also skilled, accomplished, and independent. However, the geisha realized embodying femininity was equally important as her accomplishments because it made her a complete woman and most desirable to men. As you work hard to look your best, enhancing your femininity is necessary to complete your beauty. Without it, your beauty will not reach its full potential. With it, all of your qualities become more attractive. If a woman has a take charge personality while also being feminine at the same time, then she is sexy and desirable. Adding a touch of femininity will make your actions more noticeable to men. Men were smitten at the sight of the feminine geisha, but they became more intrigued as they discovered that she was strong, intelligent, accomplished, and independent.

Attain classic femininity

As a female, you have been blessed with feminine traits. When cultivated, they will make you beautiful in a man's eyes. As the geisha did, tend to and highlight your feminine attributes. Do your hands appear inviting? Are you gentle in your execution? Do you speak softly? Is your speech eloquent or is it more masculine as a means of appearing to relate better to men? Do you dress with adequate femininity or are your female curves hidden? Do you wear your hair in a style that reminds a man of your femininity? From how you speak and dress to how you address men all should appear feminine.

❋ Be well groomed. Your hair should look combed and neat. Your fingers and toes should be manicured, whether done professionally or at home. Tending to your hair, fingers, and toes are essential because they emphasize your natural feminine attributes that distinguish you from a man.

❋ Wear feminine clothing and shoes, such as skirts, dresses, and high heels. When you wear pants or jeans, accessorize with a pair of high heels or nice flats. Do not wear running sneakers and sweatpants unless you are exercising. Every time you get dressed, ask yourself if you look feminine. A man prefers clothes that show that you are a woman.

❋ Avoid cursing. Feminine women do not have a foul mouth. Cursing will make you sound harsh and abrupt. Men find it unattractive and unfeminine when women curse. A man is attracted to the way a woman can naturally have a soft, kind tone of voice.

✹ Control the level of your voice by not speaking too loudly. Kyoto geisha spoke a special dialect that was much softer than the modern Japanese language because it was more attractive. A loud voice is unfeminine and is grating on a man's ears. Your voice should be eloquent.

✹ Be aware of your voice and do not allow your tone to be demanding. Be aware of the sound of your articulation. There are ways to get what you want without coming across as overly forceful. The geisha's speech was light and at ease.

✹ Be confident, but soften your confidence so it is not threatening. Confidence is a quality that men find attractive in a woman, but not so for conceit. A man likes a woman who is confident in what she does well, yet humble about her achievements.

✹ Be soft and gentle in your approach, both with how you touch, speak, and act. The way that you shake a hand, clap, and hold things should be gentle. Your touch or speech should not emulate a man. A man is attracted to you because of your feminine traits.

✹ Every time you are in the presence of a man, remember that a man does not want to date a woman who resembles one of his male friends. You will not impress a man by being masculine. Be distinct from a man. Be proud to be a woman and celebrate your femininity.

A woman must use her femininity

No matter how physically perfect a woman, she is less attractive to a man if she is not feminine. This was the case for Sam who just celebrated her thirty-fifth birthday. Sam lived with her Siamese cat in a one-bedroom apartment off of Central Park West. Without question, Sam was beautiful. She had a striking face and incredible body. She took classes in pilates, yoga, and spinning on a daily basis. Sam did anything necessary to improve and tone her physique. Some days she would go to two gym classes in one single day. If she had to work late, then she was notorious for canceling plans with friends so she could work out. The result was that Sam had a near perfect body that made many women envious.

Sam was so attractive at first sight that one would think she had men constantly asking her out, which she did. Sometimes, Sam would have three dates in one week. However, for some reason, none of these men stuck around for long. Years went by and Sam continued to run into the same dilemma – half of Sam's dates took her out only once and others ended it after a month or two. Men did not want to be in a long-term relationship with her. Sam was perplexed. With the number of dates she had been on, the odds were that one of them should have led to a serious boyfriend.

Among the men she dated, one in particular stood out from the rest – Peter. Sam especially regretted that their relationship did not advance further than a couple of months. Sam hoped Peter was *the one* because they got along great. Peter was funny and they shared many laughs together. He was athletic like her and they would go to the gym together. Peter liked to cook and eat healthy food, similar to Sam. When Peter told Sam he wanted to stop seeing her, he explained that it was because he considered Sam more of a 'friend' than a girlfriend. This made no sense to Sam. She thought that the quality time that they shared together and similar interests were what Peter wanted in a girlfriend. Plus, Sam was physically attractive. As a result, Sam convinced herself that Peter just was not ready for a commitment.

A year passed since their break up without any contact until Sam ran into Peter one day and he was with a woman who he introduced as his fiancé. Devastated, Sam asked around and found out that Peter met his now fiancé at the end of her and Peter's relationship. He had chosen this woman over her. What hurt Sam even more was that Peter was ready to get married, but just not to her. Sam did not understand. Peter's fiancé was not nearly as pretty as she was and was not in as good of shape. Though, friends who knew them both saw that Peter's fiancé was very feminine and had a light demeanor, unlike Sam. Peter's fiancé was also kind and pleasant to be around and Peter was clearly enamored by her. Sam, on the other hand, had been described by men as, "Rough around the edges. She is beautiful at first sight, but too much like a guy when you get to know her. She talks and acts like a man. She is too aggressive."

This was Sam's problem – no matter how amazing of a body Sam had or how striking of a face, it did not matter because she was not feminine enough. When Sam wanted something, she would order people around in a loud, demanding voice. She also enjoyed challenging her male peers and prided herself on being tough on the exterior. She constantly cursed, believing it made her appear as being no nonsense and in charge. Peter's fiancé was not as physically beautiful as Sam at first sight, but she was pretty enough to catch Peter's eye and noticeably more feminine in her demeanor. To Peter, this made her attractive enough that he wanted to spend the rest of his life with this woman. For Peter, like other men, his ideal woman had to be feminine.

Some women are misled because they believe that to be feminine means to give up their strength. It takes much more confidence and security to not appear aggressive and in control. The strongest woman is the woman who is comfortable with uncertainty and who does not have to prove her strength to others. When you are feminine, you are demonstrating the power you possess as a woman. This power has intrigued men and ignited their desire since the beginning of time.

Be feminine – practice *Ritual 2.*

Highlight your feminine mystique every single day. Do not allow it to be dormant. It is what differentiates you from a man and is a catalyst for enticing a man's desire for you. Your feminine mystique is the natural gift that you possess by simply being a woman. It is the softness in your voice; a gentle touch; sensual, smooth legs; and the way your eyes sparkle as you lightly laugh. It is how your hair frames your face and brushes against your neck, arousing a man's natural instinct to want the companionship of a woman. Strive to be an epitome of femininity.

[A geisha] was not so much a woman as a walking work of art, a compilation of symbols and markers of eroticism, as far removed from a human being as a bonsai is from a natural tree. Geisha have been described as icons of femininity.[4]

DEMONSTRATE SUBTLE SEX APPEAL

Subtlety

The geisha mastered the art of subtle sex appeal

The geisha perfected how to subtly attract men with her sex appeal, which was especially apparent in the *maiko* appearance. The *maiko* dress was not only feminine, it was deliberately designed to enhance her seductiveness. The *maiko* wore a special kimono called a *hikizuri* that hung much lower on her back than the standard kimono so as to reveal more of the nape of her neck and upper back. Luxurious scarlet fabric was sewn along the top edge of her kimono neckline, visibly laying against her painted white upper chest, back and shoulders. The onlooker was aroused by the sight of the *maiko's* jet black hair pulled up, revealing her neck accentuated with a loose collar draping down her back, fringed in scarlet, contrasting her white nape. The *maiko's* nape was further accentuated as two tines of white slashed up it, angling up behind her ears, leaving a sharp W of unpainted flesh arrowing down from her hairline, swooping down to her delicate shoulder blades. Calculated detail was placed on the nape to tempt a man with the erotic symbolism of exposed flesh in the shape of a W, highlighted against white contrasted with a fringe of scarlet. In Japanese sexuality, the nape of the neck is considered erogenous. It is believed to be the sexiest of all parts of the decently clothed woman.[1]

Following the time-tested tradition of the flower and willow world, the geisha of today still limit how much skin is exposed. Revealing too much of the back is considered indelicate. The sight of a scarlet-fringed kimono collar draping down the nape of a woman's neck is more tempting to a man than an exposed body. Much is left to the imagination. A man is more excited when wondering what lies beneath the kimono.[2] For centuries, the geisha has tempted men by revealing merely a small amount of skin and is considered one of the sexiest icons throughout history. She mastered the art of being subtly sexy.

Her presence and surroundings within the flower and willow world represented images of beauty and sensuality – from the traditional, elegant, yet understated wooden houses within the *hanamachi* to the *maiko* and *geiko* in their exquisite silk kimonos, floating across intimate narrow lanes; to the colorful flowers adorning the streets and the flower towns that resembled a romantic dream. Craftsmen, artists, and geisha brought the *hanamachi* to life for a few select guests so that they might have an exquisite experience. At the center of the flower towns was the geisha. She was the exquisite flower, unforgettable to men, as flowers symbolized eroticism in East Asia. A flower is delicate, soft, colorful, and fragrant – a beautiful natural image.

As the geisha and flower and willow world symbolized sensuality, you can also master the art of subtle sex appeal.

Possessing subtle sex appeal is an art. It is how you take the most sensual parts of your body and accentuate them just enough to tempt a man. It is how you move your body, speak, and look at a man. If you reveal yourself completely, then it is less exciting to a man. Yet, if you tempt a man to imagine, then he will be more intrigued. To master the art of subtle sex appeal is to tempt a man with your presence and the silhouette of your figure.

Employ subtle sexiness and mesmerize men

Men are intrigued by the women that they find sexy. This intrigue influences their sexual attraction to women. The women who are most successful with men understand how to attract men with subtle sexiness. They stand out among other women and receive much of the male attention. These women understand what it means and how to be sexy. They are sexier than others, yet are not always the prettiest. On the other hand, there are women who are naturally pretty, but do not have sex appeal. These women are not achieving their full potential of being the most desirable among all other women.

Have you ever heard a man say, "She is pretty, but she does not really do it for me." or "She could be a lot prettier, but she is too plain for my tastes." Natural physical beauty is limited to how much it can attract a man. A man wants a woman who will excite him – a woman who will make him feel like no other woman can; a woman whose voice, touch, and presence he longs for at all times. This woman has mastered the art of subtle sex appeal. She recognizes the strengths that will make her sexier and knows how to enhance them to attract a man. The art of learning to be subtly sexy is critical to arousing a man's inner passion and intrigue so that he wants to get to know more about you and ultimately become intimate.

Increasing your attractiveness and becoming sexy begins with your state of mind. If you feel you don't have the prettiest face, then do not worry. There are ways to make your face prettier, but what matters most in having subtle sex appeal is adding to your allure. Physically attractive women who are considered pretty are often flat and missing that "umph" that men seek. You can be more attractive than these women even if you feel they are naturally prettier than you. What makes a woman truly desirable is how her presence and spirit arouses a man.

Exude subtle sex appeal

Any woman can wear revealing clothing, but few women understand how to be truly alluring. What does a man find sexy? How do you tactfully catch a man's eye? What are the secrets to being sexy? Having sex appeal does not necessarily come natural to most women, but you can learn how to be subtly sexy. It can be as simple as the way you walk or glance at a man. However, the most important secret of subtle sex appeal is, as the geisha did, to reveal just enough to intrigue a man. Subtlety is the essence of the kimono mystique.[3]

❊ Accentuate your curves and wear clothes that flatter your best assets. Be careful to not cross the fine line between appearing sexy and revealing too much. Clothes that are short and skimpy can state that you are easily obtainable rather than sexy. How you dress should excite a man to want to be with you everyday rather than only one night.

❊ When you are going out, wear clothes that make you feel sexy, such as silk and cashmere, or a skirt that shows off your legs.

❋ Always wear sexy lingerie. If you are wearing sexy lingerie under your clothes, then you will feel sexier and men will be able to sense it.

❋ Soak in a tub with bath oil at least once a week. It will make your skin feel soft like silk, resulting in feeling sexier.

❋ Keep your legs, underarms, and bikini waxed or shaved. It will help you look and feel sexy.

❋ Make it a point to always smell nice. Every woman should have a scent; whether it is the shampoo or soap she uses or her favorite perfume. A woman should have a pleasant, subtle smell that is not overwhelming. Your scent should arouse a man and remind him that you are feminine and sensual.

❋ Put your body first and tend to it. The healthier you are, the sexier you will look and feel. Regardless of the size a woman's body, it should be healthy. In being so, men will view you as sexy.

❋ Invest in a book by a well-respected makeup artist or refer to their web site for tips. If makeup is worn the right way, then your face can transform from plain to sensual. Well-regarded makeup artists can teach you how to bring out your eyes and make your lips appear sexier. Your eyes and lips are among the most sensual parts of your body. The right glance can drive a man wild, while sensual lips can arouse a man's inner desire.

✿ When a man is close to you, your eyes can serve as the most powerful tool to attract men. They are the windows into your soul. A smile and sparkle in your eyes reveal the warmth in your soul. A flirtatious glance arouses a man, ignites the chase, and makes him wonder if he can have you. Eyes that gaze back at him while he speaks provides him with your undivided attention and makes him feel as if he is the only one in the room that matters to you.

✿ When a man is watching you, gracefully lead your eyes in his direction. Look at him, acknowledging that he is in your presence. Then gently move your eyes away and continue what you were doing. You have acknowledged him, but it will still be a mystery to him as to whether you are interested.

✿ Look a man in the eyes when you speak to him. Avoid fidgeting or appearing nervous. Be confident. If a beautiful woman looks a man in the eyes when she speaks, then the man feels like he is the center of the universe.

✿ Flirt with your eyes. The right glance from your eyes is more powerful than the movement of your body.

✿ When you are embarrassed, smile and laugh gently. A sexy woman is a confident woman who never falters.

✿ Being subtly sexy is a state of mind. Do whatever you can to make yourself feel sexy. If you feel sexy, then you will look sexy. A man wants to spend the rest of his life with a woman whose image excites him.

A woman should understand the importance of exuding subtle sexiness

If you are able to exude subtle sexiness, then you can increase the number of men who find you attractive. For Sam, who tended to be more masculine than feminine, this was one of her biggest obstacles and was preventing her from having success with men. Sam had plenty of dates, but the length of time she dated men had shortened drastically over time. It was rare for her to see a man for more than a few weeks. When Sam went out, she caught the eye of almost every man because she had an incredible body, but as soon as a man would talk to her it was only a matter of time before he lost interest. Sam's personality did not fit with her physique. Her aggressive nature and masculine approach overshadowed any femininity, resulting in Sam not appearing to be sexy. Sam's outer sex appeal needed to coincide with her inner sex appeal. Since Sam's demeanor was not sexy, then she could not be physically sexy.

The same holds true for looking your best. Christy, who did not take pride in her appearance, did not take care of her health or put in the effort to look her best so it was difficult for her to exude sex appeal. On the other hand, her best friend, Laurie, tended to her body, transformed her appearance, and focused on dressing sexy. Laurie wore skirts and dresses that stopped just above her knees, accompanied with high heels, which showed off enough of her legs to tempt men. She also wore tops slim enough to reveal she had a voluptuous chest, but made certain that her tops were not too tight so to leave a little something to the imagination. She had excellent posture and walked confidently, another quality that drew men to her. Laurie was both feminine and sexy in her appearance. By the way she dressed and carried herself, Laurie had created a mystique unlike other women. She was not nearly as thin as Sam, but it did not matter. Laurie was sexy, which attracts men.

Be subtly sexy – practice *Ritual 3*.

To understand how to be subtly sexy, envision the geisha. How she walked, spoke, moved her hands, and charmed men with her wit and intelligence. Utilizing the geisha as a guide, allow the art of how to be subtly sexy to become an essence of your being. Tempt a man with the sensual subtly of your dress, presence, touch, voice, and movement. You have it within you to be a woman who is like no other – tempting a man; arousing him; and having him desire all of you, both body and soul.

The geisha world is sensual. It is the world of silk on soft skin, the aroma of fresh tatami and warm sake; it is the sumptuous banquets of tiny morsels and rare delicacies from the forest and the sea.[4]

EMBODY ELEGANCE

Elegance

The geisha exemplified elegance

To become a future geisha, a young woman's training as a *minarai* had to demonstrate unparalleled elegance as she learned to gracefully perform, entertain, and communicate with guests. Dressed exquisitely, the primary job of the *minarai* was to attend *ozashiki* (private parties in the *hanamachi*). At this time, a *minarai* was required to observe and learn in preparation of becoming a first-class dancer and musician. She became familiar with the stage and *tatami* room (place geisha typically entertained) and learned to properly sit. She also learned to move gracefully in full costume. It was important that she studied the *geiko* and *maiko* who were more experienced than she. The *minarai* had to become accustomed to the flow of chat, dances, and party games among the guests. She had to elegantly present herself as they did. By observing the *geiko* and *maiko*, the *minarai* learned to become comfortable at an *ozashiki* and to gracefully express every movement. Guests of the *ozashiki* admired the elegance of the geisha and revered the flower and willow world experience as being most exquisite. During the short *minarai* training period, the *minarai* saw for the first time the workings of an *ochaya* (teahouse where *ozashiki* were hosted). Her initial training was primarily spent at a single *ochaya*, called a *minarai-jaya*. The *minarai-jaya* Mother (owner of the *ochaya*) kept a close eye on her. Much pressure was placed on the *minarai* to become a top entertainer. Under intense scrutiny, this preparation set precedence for excellence, a trait for which the geisha carried throughout her life. It made her extremely attractive and helped her prepare for future challenges. Everyone in the *ochaya* was held to the highest standards, including the staff, but most particularly for the geisha. The *ochaya* prided itself in offering the finest and most elegant in Japanese entertainment.

When the *minarai* training ended, the *minarai* was ready to become a member of the flower and willow world as a *maiko*. Marking the event, the ceremony *san-san-kudo* (three-three-nine) was held on a lucky day. As sacred and symbolic as a wedding, the *san-san-kudo* finished with the ritual "three times three" – an exchange of thimble-sized cups between the *maiko* and her *Onesan* (Older Sister) who was carefully chosen to serve as her role model and mentor. The *maiko* and *Onesan* were bonded together by passing three cups to each other and sipping each three times.[1] The *minarai* graduated to a *maiko* and took on a new name, half of which was adopted from her *Onesan's* name. She was formally recognized as a geisha within an *okiya* and was expected to present herself as such. She transformed from being in a state of inexperience to one of elegance and grace.

The geisha was the essence of elegance, demonstrated by how she learned to elegantly dress, walk, stand, speak, pour tea, and write calligraphy. She performed every task with grace. Her script was expressive and exquisite[2] and each body movement was elegantly executed. She carefully rehearsed her motions – opening a sliding door on her knees, standing, and then closing the door again on her knees. It was essential that she learned the correct kimono to wear for each occasion and that she stood gracefully and walked softly. These were a few of the many customs that she followed to enhance her exquisiteness.[3] Men sought out the flower and willow world so that they could experience its elegance and the exquisiteness of the geisha. Today, elegance seems to be a lost art preserved by the geisha and a small number of women who stand out to men. It is rare to see a truly elegant woman – a woman who is classy and timeless.

Possessing elegance is a quality that will accentuate your beauty throughout your lifetime. The geisha attracted men with her elegance, serving as an example of how to elegantly present yourself. Exhibiting elegance shows that you are refined and dignified. When you move gracefully, you are also indicating to the world that you are confident and poised. Men are attracted to a woman who gracefully presents herself as being self-assured. She is comfortable with herself and has a sense of purpose, yet her execution is soft and unthreatening to men. An elegant woman is an example to follow. She is admired and desired by men.

Present elegance and become a unique woman

Today, most of the women glorified in the media are flashy and abrupt. They often make poor decisions and their motivation is typically to draw attention to themselves. This small group has worldwide exposure and, unfortunately, serves as a role model for other women. It is not uncommon to see women today admiring these celebrities and trying to emulate them. However, most men do not find this type of woman attractive, particularly as a lifelong partner. The geisha was a celebrity in her time and the antithesis of most modern day celebrities. Her elegance was valued by men for centuries and even is to this day.

When you elegantly present yourself, you are not shouting out for attention. Yet, men will notice you. When you are elegant, there is beauty in your every movement. You are exhibiting class, poise, and grace. Equally important, you are also making yourself exclusive. When you gracefully move, you are revealing a glimpse of your refined beauty that a man must pursue in order to know more. When you elegantly present yourself, you do not act abrupt and are careful not to reveal too much about yourself. The geisha was the image of beauty and elegance. Little has been revealed about her over the centuries because the flower and willow world was a private world that existed only in exclusivity. By being elegant, you are showing a glimpse into your refined beauty that few men will have the privilege of knowing.

Exemplify elegance

To embody elegance, you must constantly be aware of how you dress, move, sit, stand, and speak. Do your clothes flatter your body and fit you properly? Are they tasteful? Do you have excellent posture? Do you walk gracefully? When you speak, do you annunciate clearly and softly? Is your speech thoughtful and deliberate, yet light? When you walk into a room, do you appear refined? Being elegant, while simultaneously feminine and subtly sexy, is to become the image men passionately desire.

❋ Be poised. An elegant woman is always poised, whether it is how she stands or speaks. She is in control and articulate. An elegant woman is a sophisticated woman.

❋ Have good posture – stand and sit up straight. A geisha was never supposed to slouch.[4] If you have excellent posture, then you will look taller and your silhouette will be more attractive. Yoga, pilates, and dance can help improve your posture.

❋ Be graceful and at ease when you walk. The correct way to walk in a kimono has been described as never stomping, but instead moving softly to echo the way the heart beats, as in Zen.[5]

❋ Dress well. To be elegant, a woman must dress well. The geisha wore the finest kimonos and was the essence of elegance.

❋ Tailor clothing to correctly fit your body. Do not roll up your pants because they are too long or use a belt because your skirt is too loose. An elegant woman uses a belt as an accessory and her clothes fit her perfectly.

❋ Exemplify class. There are women who are showy and endlessly gossip about others and money. A truly elegant woman would never engage in this type of behavior.

❋ Be articulate. Be concise with your words and speak clearly and slowly. Avoid saying *um*. Speak eloquently with purpose and do not ramble. An elegant woman has a voice that men notice.

❋ Exhibit grace in your movement and speech. An elegant woman is never rough in her execution. The geisha kneeled and rose elegantly and opened sliding doors with a discreet motion of her hands, fingers, and thumbs held straight and pressed together.[6]

Elegance can transcend a woman's beauty

The geisha refined each detail of her being by consciously focusing attention on her presence. She elegantly presented herself because she understood that it made her more beautiful and attractive to men. It is this detail of possessing elegance that will enhance your attractiveness. Valerie, who lived in Boston in her early forties, had always struggled with how to present herself in a soft, non-confrontational manner. When Valerie spoke, she did so forcefully. When she moved, it was as if she was determined to get her way. Even when Valerie wore dresses that clung to her attractive body, she lacked the elegance necessary for the dress to fully flatter her. Valerie's mannerisms were not graceful and they took away from the loveliness of the dresses. A dress can appear elegant on a mannequin or a hanger, but if an elegant woman does not wear it, then it becomes less elegant. Imagine an ordinary woman in a geisha's kimono, a woman with little knowledge of the geisha. If a woman is not as graceful as the geisha, then the kimono is more exquisite by itself. The clothes should accent the woman and not the opposite.

The geisha's beauty was more intriguing because she moved with grace and poise. Her touch was gentle and she walked softly. She wore her kimonos elegantly. Her practice of perfect posture and training in dance gave her the ability to be graceful in her execution. Every action that the geisha performed, whether it was a dance, song, or tea ceremony, was done elegantly. Her trademark was her beauty and elegance. Today, there are few elegant women left as Valerie serves as being more of the norm. Being elegant has become a lost art. For centuries men have appreciated the beauty of elegance.

Be elegant – practice *Ritual 4.*

Watching an elegant woman is like watching a woman dance to a beautiful song. The geisha was graceful when she moved, thoughtful when she spoke, and humbly self-assured. She was smooth around the edges and she transcended her beauty to a higher level. Her exquisiteness was natural, an essence of her entire being. A glorious vision of beauty to a man – this is the woman you should become.

In the flower towns, every guest can fancy himself a romantic prince of the fabulously elegant, decadent Heian Era. The teahouse provides the setting and the geisha is the catalyst. The fantasy may never be satisfied but it is all the more exquisite for that. [7]

EXHIBIT INTELLIGENCE AND ACCOMPLISHMENT

Achievement

The geisha modeled intellect and accomplishment

Men consistently sought out the geisha's beauty, but it was because of her intelligence and great artistic accomplishments that she mesmerized men. The word geisha literally means artist – (gei) meaning *art* and (sha) meaning *person* or *doer.* The geisha was committed to refining and improving her artistic skills. She could not hold the title of geisha unless she did so. A geisha from the city of Kyoto could spend up to six years as a *maiko* training in a teahouse, and studying traditional dance, song, music, and other refined arts so that she could perform at a professional level. No other single profession required the range of expertise in traditional Japanese arts as was expected of a Kyoto geisha.[1]

From the moment a geisha debuted as a *maiko*, she began performing at the arduous annual round of spectacular public performances, festivals, and events. On a daily basis she took dance and music classes at the *kaburenjo*. With rigorous practice, her performance style gradually improved. At the heart of her practice was the goal of reaching perfection and becoming a top artist in Japan. She was also expected to perfect the tea ceremony. At her young age as a *maiko*, she was not yet expected to master the art of conversation. This came with experience. Regular guests at an *ochaya* most often preferred to converse with a *geiko* who was older and more learned. When evening came, the *maiko* attended *ozashiki* at the *ochaya* starting at six o'clock. Parties went late into the night where *maiko* and *geiko* would exhibit their talents, including performing music and dance, leading games, and initiating witty and engaging conversation. With only a few hours of sleep, the *maiko* began her morning again with dance and music classes.[2]

After she lived and trained in the *hanamachi* for five years or longer, she graduated from a senior *maiko* to a full-fledged *geiko*. When the time came to graduate to a *geiko*, the scarlet fabric sewn along the neckline of her kimono was almost buried under silver – a signal that she was ready to transition from trainee to master. She worked tirelessly to improve her artistic talents and hopefully built a strong network of contacts and guests. Many senior *maiko* chose not to become a full-fledged *geiko* and ended their careers as a geisha. A devotion to beauty, artistry, and intellect set them apart, which resulted in the senior *maiko* being in high demand. Some senior *maiko* who did not become *geiko* learned enough so that they were able to make a respectable living in the world of refined *asobi* (entertainment) anywhere in Japan. Other senior *maiko* decided to marry and settle down, often with elite men from the sports or political worlds. Politicians were grateful for the vast network of contacts their former *maiko* spouses could provide. Senior

maiko and *geiko* of the *hanamachi* Gion Kobu were especially prized as wives for rich and powerful men because of their beauty, sophistication, achievements, and connections.[3]
  For the senior *maiko* who chose to follow the path of the *geiko*, her promotion was formalized with the *erikae* ceremony. The symbolic scarlet collar was unstitched and replaced with a white one. As a *geiko*, she was no longer expected to make it on aesthetics alone. From now on, her power of personality and artistic skills were valued most. Her physical beauty was not as important as it was when she was a *maiko* because she will become more intriguing and attractive as she possesses great talent and refined intelligence. Her dress changed to a style that was much more conservative than the elaborate *maiko* dress. Her kimono no longer hung provocatively low on her nape and her hair changed to a more subdued style. Her platform *okobo* clogs were replaced with less flamboyant *zori* sandals and *geta* clogs. Still, as a *geiko* she was instantly recognizable as her style, elegance, and sophistication were a world apart from the norm. She had now mastered the art of conversation and was expected to be current on the latest news and well versed on conversation. Her profession depended on her ability to converse with politicians and keep secrets. Men entertained at an *ochaya* because they could trust the *geiko* on the most secretive matters.[4] The *geiko* served as a confidant and was the friend of Japan's most powerful men. Some of these friendships lasted a lifetime.
  The highest standards of artistry, etiquette, and poise were demanded of the *geiko*. She was revered as a professional artist and was no longer allowed to make mistakes in the repertoire like with the case when she was a *maiko*. As a *geiko*, she was usually established in a specialized role as either a *tachikata* (dancer) or *jikata* (musician). *Tachikata* tended to be more beautiful and the stars were in constant demand. Their schedules could be booked up months in advance and they spent

only short periods of time at each party. They made substantial earnings and tips by performing at multiple *ochaya* in an evening. The geisha's time was charged in units, from five to thirty minutes depending on the *hanamachi*, but guests were expected to pay a full fee for a *geiko* no matter the amount of time she spent at a party. *Jikata* tended to earn less, but their profession was steadier. Older *jikata* who were expert players of the *shamisen* were always in strong demand.[5]

As the geisha's achievements were admired and appreciated whether she was twenty or forty years old, you should establish substance underneath your physical beauty and differentiate yourself from other women so that you stand out to men. Now that you have refined your outer beauty, you must take the steps to perfect your inner beauty. Otherwise, you risk a man becoming bored and losing interest over the long-term. Men were intrigued by and attracted to the geisha well into her older years as she became more learned and artistically talented. Every woman is capable of broadening her knowledge and increasing her accomplishments if she is willing to exercise her mind and challenge herself. The geisha did this by perfecting her dance, song, and musical talents. She was also an expert in conversation, performing tea ceremonies, calligraphy, flower arranging, and reciting haiku and waka poetry. In Japan, the geisha was most recognized and revered for her talent and great artistic accomplishments.

Show intelligence and accomplishment and be loved for your inner qualities

The geisha's beauty is a window that revealed great intellect and talent. As a professional performer, her appearance mattered, but without mastering her art, she could not be a geisha. She earned the title of geisha through her hard work in becoming a superior artist. The geisha proved that a woman does not have to appear brainless and unskilled to be the object of desire for men. On the contrary, men sought out the geisha because of her achievements and sharp mind. She was recognized among the most talented artists in Japan. Some geisha became famous musicians and dancers, equivalent to modern day movie stars.

Following the geisha's devotion to her art, you should work hard at making yourself uniquely intelligent and accomplished. Your intelligence will intrigue a man and enthuse him to desire your constant companionship. If you exhibit intelligence and continue to be accomplished, then you possess long-term desirability. A man wants to be with a woman with whom he can intelligently converse. He wants to admire her accomplishments because a woman with achievements is more intriguing and exciting. He will not be bored.

Demonstrate intelligence and accomplishment

Everyone possesses skills that they do well. Every day, work on sharpening your mind and improving your talents. Recognize your strengths and build on them. In what ways are you accomplished? What is it that you do best? What distinguishes you from other women? Set yourself apart and differentiate yourself from other women. There are many men who are ready for a serious girlfriend or marriage. They simply cannot find a woman who they can envision being with in the long-term.

❋ The geisha was well read and current on the latest news so that she could converse intelligently with men. Try to increase your knowledge so that you can speak with men on many levels.

❄ The geisha studied traditional instruments, such as the *shamisen, shakuhachi,* and drums. She also studied traditional Japanese songs, traditional dances, the tea ceremony, literature, and poetry. Similar to the geisha, have unique interests.

❄ The geisha was incredibly disciplined and spent years, sometimes decades, perfecting her artistic and musical skills. Most of a *maiko's* time was occupied with practice. She was expected to learn how to sing, play musical instruments, perform the tea ceremony, and dance exquisitely.[6] To be accomplished, you must practice and be committed in the long-term – mastering a skill does not happen instantaneously.

❄ The geisha typically had a skill that she did exceptionally well, such as dance or playing a musical instrument. Rather than trying to perfect everything, use your time wisely and focus on what you do best. The more accomplished you become at one skill, the more you will stand out to men.

❄ The geisha was humble about her achievements. While it is important to have interests and accomplishments, remember to remain humble. You are more attractive to men if you are humble (*Ritual 6* Exercise Humility in Everything You Do).

What kind of a beautiful woman are you?

There are different types of beautiful women. There is the beautiful woman who turns men's heads, but loses credibility when she speaks because she appears to lack intelligence. Then there is the beautiful woman who turns men's heads and interests them even more because of what she offers beneath her physical beauty. These women are rare, and for that reason, all the more attractive to men. In any cosmopolitan city, you can find beautiful women with no substance. However, men are hoping to find a gem – the woman who they desire physically and who also intrigues them. They want to hear her speak and care about what she has to say because she is beautiful, interesting, and intelligent.

Tina was one of these rare gems. She lived in San Francisco and worked as an editor. She regularly published articles and was writing a book. In her free time, she traveled around the world, visiting museums and exploring the culture and architecture of faraway cities. Her favorite interests ranged from reading to traveling and collecting art. She was a beautiful blonde with bright blue eyes. She was full of energy and passionate about life. Tina was the sort of woman that one could never imagine being single, which she never was for very long. When she broke up with her boyfriends, there was always another great guy eagerly waiting. Men would constantly ask Tina's friends about her. "Is she single? Do you think she would go out with me?" What set Tina apart from other women is that men not only wanted to go on a date with Tina, they also wanted to have her as a girlfriend. Like Tina, you want to set yourself apart with your intelligence and accomplishments, making you more desirable to men than other women.

Be intelligent and accomplished – practice *Ritual 5*.

What lies beneath your physical beauty matters. If you cannot speak intelligently about interesting subjects or do not have any noteworthy accomplishments, then you offer very little to stimulate a man over time. Your inner beauty must be as attractive and intriguing as your outer beauty, if not more. Men are drawn to many aspects of a woman. You should first look your best to initially grab a man's attention, but you must also have substance beneath the surface. What lies within you is what will increase a man's desire to be with only you and want to spend a lifetime with you.

Geisha are highly trained professionals in the fields of traditional Japanese dance, music, and tea ceremony. Most crucially of all, they command in full the etiquette, deportment, and repartee which form a very special Japanese aesthetic called iki. Ultra-aesthetic but playful and witty, iki refers to a highly cultivated but not solemn sensibility, as open to broad jokes and puns as it is deeply versed in traditional high arts. Top-class geisha are living embodiments of iki. [7]

EXERCISE HUMILITY IN EVERYTHING YOU DO

Humility

The geisha always acted with humility

Humility is deeply ingrained in the Japanese culture. This is exhibited through the Japanese belief that there is one perfect set way of doing anything, which is defined in the arts as a *kata* (set form). The most celebrated example for the geisha was the way in which she kneeled to slide a door open and closed when she entered a room. Every aspect of her posture was set, from the angle at which her arm was held to the position of her knees on the floor. The *kata* was not memorized repetition. Instead, it was performed with humble consciousness as an expression of respect for the guest and for the geisha's role as a host. According to the Japanese arts, where the body leads, the heart follows. This philosophy is based from Zen

Buddhism – constant, controlled repetition of the same task allows the practitioner to break through the barrier of the ego and discard its trappings.[1]

The geisha had many achievements of which to be proud. However, from the beginning of her tutelage, she was taught and expected to remain humble. When an aspiring future geisha moved into an *okiya* and began her *shikomi* apprentice, she started at the lowest level within a strict hierarchy and was expected to humbly accept her place. Every girl in her community was her older sister until a new one arrived. She had to drop to her knees and bow whenever an older sister entered the room.[2] As a *shikomi*, she scrubbed the floors, and at the end of the day, she sat waiting in the entrance vestibule of the *okiya* for the *geiko* and *maiko* to return from the *ochaya*. Despite it often being two in the morning or later, she was expected to properly greet her seniors and wait as they each bathed. Baths were taken in order of rank and the *shikomi* went last. A few hours later she had to be up in the morning to begin her day. Backbreaking labor and sleep deprivation were part of every Japanese apprenticeship and believed to be necessary to mold an individual into a future master of art. For the *shikomi*, the hope of transforming into a beautiful *maiko* motivated her to keep going.

When she earned the title of geisha, discarding her ego and practicing humility was an essential element for mastering her art. To begin a dance class, the geisha was required to take her *maioghi* (dancing fan) out of her *obi* with her right hand and place it horizontally on the floor, between herself and her teacher, and bow. This motion was a highly ritualistic and symbolic act indicating that the geisha was leaving the ordinary world behind and was ready to receive the teacher's expertise. Knowledge was then passed from the dance teacher to the student through the process of *mane*. The famous geisha, Mineko Iwasaki, described the meaning of *mane* as "We repeat the movements of our teachers until we can duplicate them exactly, until, in a sense, we have absorbed the teacher's mastery into ourselves. Artistic technique must be fully integrated into the cells of our bodies if we are to use it to express what is in our hearts, and this takes many years of practice."[3]

Only with time, practice, and a humble ego could a geisha become a world-class performer. This was exhibited by the *tachikata* geisha who studied a form of unmasked *Noh* dance. *Nihon Buyo* is a stately, graceful dance form in which even an elderly expert practitioner can appear as beautiful as a young *maiko*. In *Nihon Buyo*, self-expression is not the aim. The purpose is perfect execution of *kata* (set form). The more the practitioner matures and masters the art, the more powerful the performance. For this reason, *tachikata* geisha did not need to retire young. They could continue working well past their youth. It is also why the depth of the geisha goes far beyond the surface image of the geisha as an exotic, young dancer recognized for her physical beauty.[4]

To this day both *maiko* and *geiko* are expected to be committed professionals, dedicated to mastering their skills and art. There is still great pride in being taught by the best teachers in Japan. With long periods of practice, a *tachikata geiko* may reach the equivalent of master status in Japanese dance called *natori* (the highest form of art). In the tradition of the flower and willow world, the modern *geiko's* practice is founded on the *kata*. Reaching master status can only be achieved with a humble mind. An even greater achievement than your accomplishments is reaching success while remaining humble. Humility is one of the most admirable qualities you can possess.

Demonstrate humility and men will be more attracted to you

It is tempting to want to gloat about your intelligence and accomplishments, but no one wants to hear about your excessive superiority and success – especially a man. This does not mean that you have to shy away from displaying your intelligence. On the contrary, you should be interesting and accomplished. However, you should show it in a humble manner. If a woman is not humble, then it can be difficult for a man to envision being in a serious relationship with her. Those who are humble are more pleasant to be around, resulting in one's achievements being greater and admired.

To exhibit humility in all of your actions indicates that you are mature and have a strong sense of self-worth. You do not seek out recognition because you do not need it to feel validated. It is the act of achieving your best through hard work that is rewarding to you. Your achievements are to better yourself and to master your art. The beauty within your art, which is admired by men, is what you have humbly accomplished throughout your lifetime.

Exhibit humble behavior

Reflect on yourself and how you can change to be more humble. How can you approach life in a different manner? How do you come across to others? When you do something well, do you have to tell someone? Do you like to tell others when you made a materialistic purchase? Do you feel good about yourself when you achieve more than others? How can you put your ego aside? Being humble requires you to be constantly aware of what you say and how you say it.

❋ Be humble about your accomplishments and careful about how you convey your achievements to others.

Many men feel successful women can come across as arrogant and entitled. A man measures his self-worth from his own accomplishments and does not want to feel that he is in competition with the woman in his life.

❀ Be real and down-to-earth. It is tempting to get caught up in a moment and draw too much attention to yourself. A woman should distinguish herself. A man wants to be in a relationship with a woman who is real.

❀ Do not appear materialistic. Be humble about what you have and what you desire. Avoid talking about money or wanting expensive items. Material objects should not define your identity.

❀ Be conscious of your words and do not brag. It is easy to find people who enjoy bragging about how much money they make or how successful they are. Even though others gloat, it does not mean that you should do it too. Society may glorify consumption, but you are more attractive if you are conscious of what is appropriate.

❀ You never want to appear as if you think that you are better than or superior to others. Geisha were taught to serve all honored guests equally and without discrimination.[5]

❀ Do not feel that you have to impress a man. By embodying the qualities of the geisha, he is already impressed.

The Rituals must be practiced with humility

Many modern women are not aware of the importance of being humble because humility is not a quality that is highly valued by society. However, if you are not humble, then you could be preventing men from taking an interest in you. This was the case for Brenda, a single woman approaching forty and living in London. Brenda seemed like the ideal modern woman. She was attractive and held a high-powered media job. She had graduated from the best universities with multiple degrees. She volunteered for charities in her free time and served on the boards of two nonprofit organizations, trying to make a difference in the world. People who knew Brenda respected her accomplishments and believed her heart was in the right place, but not everyone liked being in Brenda's company. When she talked about her achievements and goals, she would brag and look down on others she viewed as less intelligent and less accomplished than she – especially men.

Over the past ten years, Brenda was dumbfounded as to why she was not married or could not even find a decent man to be her boyfriend. She convinced herself that men were intimidated by her success and really preferred to be with a woman who was not especially smart. Brenda was pretty, successful, and intelligent. In theory, she had everything a man could and would want. Brenda's reasoning for why she was still single was not actually the case. There were plenty of great men who were interested in Brenda when they first met her, including men who were more successful than she, but the universal response from men was that Brenda was overly self-assured and conceited. Brenda could not find one single man who was equal to her in accomplishments and who actually admired her. The men who were less successful than she found Brenda to be unbearable because she made them feel inferior for not being as accomplished. It was disheartening to watch Brenda fail with men because she seemed to have all of the qualities needed to be a man's ideal female companion, except that she did not understand the importance of humility. In needing to feel accepted, Brenda wrongly assumed that she had to brag to get men to notice her.

Men want to be with an intelligent and accomplished woman, but being humble is just as important, if not more important. Achievements matter less to a man if a woman is not humble. There are many women who are not as successful or as pretty as Brenda who are in serious relationships or married. It is not because a man prefers to be with a less accomplished or less intelligent woman. It is because most men place a greater value on humility.

Be humble – practice *Ritual 6*.

Your accomplishments will have greater merit if they are achieved with humility. In the same way the geisha humbly perfected her art, each step you take to better yourself must be implemented with humility at the core. By doing so, you will become the most desirable creature to a man. Let a man uncover your intelligence and accomplishments through his own inquiries. By doing so, you will create a mystique about you that is waiting to be discovered and desired.

Here [in Japan] they say it's best to act as if you know nothing, but actually be really clever. To act as if you know everything is the worst.[6]

ACT WITH KINDNESS

Kindness

The geisha was always kind

Harmony was prized above any other social value in the flower and willow world. The geisha created harmony by being gracious and pleasant to all of the people who were an integral part of her world. This included the other geisha living in her *okiya* and people who worked in the *hanamachi*, but foremost, the geisha did her best to be gracious to all of her guests. It was important that she did not discriminate and was always happy to be at an *ozashiki*. Her role was to entertain the host of the *ozashiki* and his or her guests. When a geisha entered an *ozashiki*, the geisha was required to go over and converse with whomever was seated in the place of honor. Her expression had to read, "I could not wait to come right over and speak to you." Regardless of how she felt, it was her duty to be excited to see the person. To be a geisha meant that she made people feel good. She found likeable traits in everyone.[1] If she did not, then she failed as a geisha. Even with the guests who were not her favorites, she was cordial, engaged, and treated each one of them graciously. Her words created a welcoming environment for all in her presence and put her in the right mindset to perform her best as an artist.

Ozashiki were small and intimate, with guests, who were mostly men, but sometimes women, developing long-term close relationships with the *ochaya* and the geisha of whom they were the fondest. Traditionally, guests were usually aficionados of the arts and students of the *shamisen*, traditional art, or Japanese dance. They were trained to understand the talents of the geisha, and they enjoyed engaging in artistic dialogue. Discussions were typically devoted to current events, literature, and traditional art forms. These were the ideal guests and whom the geisha originally aimed to entertain through her engaging conversation and by showcasing her superior artistic talents.[2] The strong relationships that the geisha had with her guests first came to exist from the harmonious world she created with her kindness. Experiencing her art and intelligence, these relationships developed into deeper ones as the geisha facilitated a meeting of the minds between her and her guests.

With every action of the geisha, there was an undertone of kindness. Whether she was graciously greeting a guest, humbly serving a drink, or conversing with a guest, she was pleased to be with the guest and hoped that her words and actions made the guest feel good. In the same way the geisha's kindness lead to meaningful, long-lasting relationships, you must understand the influence that kindness plays when developing a relationship with a man. A woman who is consistently and genuinely kind will easily maintain long-term relationships with those around her. When you express kindness to a man through your words and intent from the first moment that you speak to him, you are creating a bond with him and building the base for a future relationship.

Be genuinely kind and leave a memorable impression on a man

Being kind may seem simple on the surface, but kindness goes beyond just saying nice words. What matters most is your intent and the effort that you put into it. Some women say the right things, but there is not depth to their words and their intentions are self-serving. When a man is hoping to meet a woman who could be his life partner, he is especially astute to the women around him. He seeks a woman who is truly kind from the heart and whose words have meaning. If your priority is to get married, then most men will see through your intentions and recognize your lack of truthfulness. Successful men are especially astute to false values and most of them make it a point to avoid women who seek men for material gains. When you express kindness, your words and actions must be genuine with your heart and mind being in the right place. When you do or say something nice, it should not be for the purpose of personally satisfying or benefitting you. You should do so because you want to compliment someone or make those around you feel good.

It is especially important that you express your kind thoughts to a man. Some individuals have difficulty express-ing kindness to others when they are truly kind hearted and have good intentions. This can be due to a variety of rea-sons, such as shyness or a busy life with little or no time to acknowledge others. Alternatively, there are people who are genuinely outright nice and their kindness is recognizable by others. The same holds true for how women appear to men. There are some women who naturally come across as kind during the first impression, while others are shy, guarded, or preoccupied and it takes time to unravel their layers to dis-cover their kindness. For a woman to make an impression on a man, there needs to be aspects of you that men should take their time to discovery (some mystery). Yet, kindness is not a quality that should take time to discover. Genuine kindness is a quality men want to see in a woman right away. You should be exhibiting this from the moment you meet a man. It is a value that is good to practice in all aspects of your life. If you are genuinely kind, then others will recognize and appreciate it, especially men. Men desire a life partner whose heart is caring and pure.

Demonstrate kindness with your words and actions

Everyone can make an effort to act and speak from a place of kindness. Few of us can say that we are truly nice to everyone all of the time. Often, most people are not conscious of when they are being unkind. How often do you criticize others and not even know that you are doing so? Do you enjoy gossiping? Do you find yourself unintentionally judging people? Do you laugh at others' expense more often than you should? These actions may seem harmless at the time, but they spark negative thoughts and unkindness. Following the way of the geisha, you should make a conscious effort to be nice because speaking and acting from a good place will enhance your beauty. Men will be attracted to the positive energy that you radiate, making your presence stand out among others.

❋ Try to be nice and pleasant all of the time. There are women who pride themselves on being tough and difficult, saying it is because they have high standards and want a man to work to get them. However, the more unpleasant you are, the less men will be attracted to you. Be nice and let a man pursue you.

❋ Avoid gossiping. Try not to say bad or negative things about other people. It is unkind and can induce bad karma. Just as important, men find a woman unattractive when she gossips.

❄ Think before you speak. Your words can hurt more than you realize. Be sensitive to the feelings of others. Plus, hurt feelings can come back to haunt you.

❄ Be conscious and try not to criticize him. This may seem obvious, but many women are unaware when they are being critical. Sharp responses such as, "Why would you do that?" or "I do not like that" are not well received.

❄ Try not to focus on negative qualities, but rather look for the good qualities in others. Do not expect the men you date to be perfect. Focus on a man's best traits because the ones you do not care for now may be less significant in a few years.

❄ If you have a boyfriend, then make a point to say at least one nice thing to him every day. It is an easy way to contribute to the relationship in a positive manner. Both of you will be happier.

❄ Try to be positive and create good energy rather than being negative. Everyone prefers to be around a positive person. Despite your great appearance, being positive will make you even more likeable.

❄ In everything you do, approach life with kind intentions.

A man is sensitive to criticism, especially from a woman

Maria, who was in her thirties and living in Brooklyn Heights, was frustrated with being single. Recently, fewer men were asking her out on a second date, and she did not understand why. In the past, Maria had her moments. Often she was too blunt and sometimes felt the need to tell her dates what she really thought. Though lately she seemed to lose all sense of what was appropriate. Maria was certain that her remarks to men were not harsh. She was doing her dates a favor by telling them what she believed to be the truth. On one occasion she told a date that he should consider finding another career because his job did not seem very promising. As one would expect, the man did not ask Maria out again. She was actually surprised and disappointed because she liked him. Maria's viewpoint was that her date had more potential than what his job offered and she thought she was doing the right thing by saying so.

This was just one example of the type of advice or criticisms that Maria shared with her dates. It was not unusual for her to tell a man, "I do not like this restaurant," or "Too bad you do not make it to the gym more often." All of her comments were directed towards a man's personal choices. Maria actually believed that her remarks were helpful and could not understand why men did not want to hear them. Although Maria was beautiful and smart, her looks and brains could only take her so far. A man wants to hear words that are kind and encouraging. Even if there are things about a man that you initially do not particularly like, your opinion may change over time and as you get to know him better. Maybe a man does not exercise a lot because he is working long hours and trying to build a career so that he can support a family in the future. Or maybe it took him hours to pick out a restaurant for your date even though it did not live up to the reviews. Try to find the good in every circumstance and channel your criticisms into positive thoughts so that when you speak you are coming from a place of kindness. When you have an opinion, you can express it in a way that is sensitive to others.

Be kind – practice *Ritual 7*.

Similar to the flower and willow world, you want to create a harmonious, non-confrontational, pleasant environment when you are with a man. Like the geisha, you have it within you to make a man feel wonderful so that you feel good in return. Your heart must know how to speak and act from a place free of criticism and judgment. When you speak and act, a man should feel good as if he is in a special place, a place where he will be greeted with kind words and love. This is ultimately what every man wants – to be encouraged and showered with kindness.

A first-class geiko uses all the skill at her command to please her audience, to make every person she comes in contact with feel wonderful.[3]

PERFORM THOUGHTFUL ACTS

Generosity

The geisha always demonstrated thoughtfulness

To be a geisha meant that the geisha demonstrated her kindness through thoughtful acts. When she entertained, she was attentive to her guests and made each feel appreciated. She developed a strong bond with them by looking after them and ensuring that they had a wonderful experience.[1] She knew her guests well and personalized the *ozashiki* to each guest of honor. This meant initiating conversations around a guest's interests and knowing their favorite dances. The geisha was an expert in the art of timing so that there was never a dull moment. She made sure that the *ozashiki* seamlessly moved from conversation to tea ceremony to dance performance. All was done to ensure that the guest of honor and his or her guests had a one-of-a-kind experience that was created solely by the geisha, which could only be found in the flower and willow world.

A common misconception of the flower and willow world is that it catered only to men. While most guests were men, women still hosted *ozashiki* and often attended them as guests. Some men brought their wives and children so that they too could experience the dance and music performances. Young adult children of guests also attended *ozashiki* as part of their education. A family could have a relationship with an *ochaya* that spanned generations. The famous geisha, Mineko Iwasaki, recalled that she often knew a guest's entire family. Guests held *ozashiki* for family reunions or a grandfather hosted an *ozashiki* for his newborn grandchild. To show her guests that she cared about them and their families, Mineko Iwasaki took the extra step of remembering over a hundred of her guest's birthdays, their wives' birthdays, and their wedding anniversaries. [2]

Exhibiting thoughtfulness was one of the reasons the geisha gained loyalty and developed friendships with many of her guests. There was much greatness to be uncovered beneath her mystical beauty. Guests enjoyed and appreciated her thoughtful acts, which demonstrated her vast depth. Underneath the aesthetic of the geisha was a personal connection that lasted decades. The geisha had a loyal base of guests who requested her over and over. Her thoughtful acts built bonds with guests, resulting in the guests desiring to spend more time with her. Similarly, you should demonstrate the same thoughtfulness. Each thoughtful gesture is a step towards creating a bond with a man. He will feel a personal connection and will appreciate that you went out of your way for him.

Show thoughtfulness and be appreciated by a man

As you begin to cultivate a relationship with a man, thoughtful gestures will help you stand out among others. Typically, the man is taking you out and planning dates, often making most of the effort to spend time together. When you have an opportunity, perform a thoughtful gesture in return because it is the right thing to do. It does not need to be extravagant. Extravagance does not make you anymore thoughtful because its value may be immaterial. You also do not want to overwhelm a man or appear smothering. Your thoughtful gestures should be small and simple. These are the most noticeable because they add a personal touch.

Everyday there are opportunities around you to be thoughtful. It is as simple as a sincere thank you note, whether it is a written email or an even more personal handwritten note. It is buying someone a bottle of wine or small box of chocolates after they do something nice for you or go out of their way to help you. It is offering to pick up lunch for your friend while you are out getting your own lunch. It is remembering to send a birthday card to a friend or calling to wish him or her a happy birthday. It is buying a book for a friend that you thought he or she would find particularly interesting. Each act should be subtle with an extra touch that will make a difference. A thoughtful gesture has greater value to a man if the effort is personalized.

Demonstrate thoughtfulness

With many modern women working full time, often they do not have time to go out of their way for others. Some women feel doing something extra for a man appears yielding and compromises their independence. On the contrary, being thoughtful actually demonstrates purpose, sophistication, and maturity. When you are thoughtful, you are aware of others and respond in a mature, sophisticated manner. It is important to perform thoughtful acts when in a relationship whether it is the initial stage or you have been with a man for years. Even though a man is independent like you, he appreciates and admires the qualities of a thoughtful woman. In the same way that the geisha looked after her guests, your thoughtfulness will be appreciated and make you more attractive to a man.

❋ If you are stopping for coffee on your way to see him, then offer to get him coffee as well. You can never be too busy to do something as little as picking up coffee for him.

❋ Do at least one thoughtful act a day for the man you love. It can be as simple as hanging up his coat or bringing home his favorite dessert.

❋ In return for all of the lovely dates he has taken you out on, get him a personal gift in return. Examples are purchasing a book about one of his favorite subjects, a bottle of wine from one of his favorite winemakers, or tickets to see his favorite sports team play. As an alternative, you could cook him his favorite dinner.

❋ Holidays and birthdays are important. Make sure you do something extra special and thoughtful. These are the times you should go out of your way for him.

❋ Surprise him by doing something special when he least expects it.

❋ Never ask for credit for your efforts. A man who is worthy of you will show his appreciation. If he is unresponsive to your thoughtfulness, then he probably is not as interested as he should be. Most likely there is someone better out there for you who will be ecstatic to be on the receiving end of your thoughtful gestures.

A woman must be sure to always show she values the man in her life

Being thoughtful is a way of life that will make you a better woman and improve your relationships with others. In close relationships, whether they are friendships or romantic, being thoughtful keeps the relationship strong and establishes a long-term bond. Caroline, a woman in her late thirties living in New York City's West Village, did not understand the true meaning of being thoughtful. This was a challenge she dealt with in her relationships. She worked in public relations and kept her free time packed with social plans. Every night she was out with her friends at restaurants and parties. Her overbooked schedule drove her boyfriend, Jake, crazy. Even though she included him in her plans, her work and personal obligations always came first. Jake respected that Caroline had to devote most of her week to work, as Jake did as well. However, with Caroline's social plans, Jake was starting to feel like he was an accessory. He questioned if Caroline was with him purely for the sake of having a boyfriend. Although Caroline would tell Jake that he was great, Jake wanted Caroline to treat him special and show him that he was just as important to her as her social life and work. On Jake's birthday, Caroline made dinner plans that day and bought an insignificant gift right before the dinner. For their anniversary, she did not even bother to buy a present until two weeks after their anniversary had passed.

Jake cared about Caroline and thought he wanted to spend the rest of his life with her. Though, before he could move their relationship forward and propose to Caroline, he wanted to see that she truly cared for him by going out of her way. If he was going to spend the rest of his life with Caroline, then he wanted his future wife to treat him well. For Caroline, it was not that she did not love Jake, it was that she was always on the go and unconscious of the fact that she was not especially considerate or generous. She became accustomed to always having Jake there for her and she did not think that she had to bother with being thoughtful. Caroline felt that telling Jake she loved him was enough. However, Jake was like most men – he wanted Caroline to show that she loved him through her actions. Otherwise, he could not marry her.

If a woman is thoughtful, then a man desires to be and spend time with her. As an example for all women, it would not have been hard for Caroline to plan in advance for Jake's birthday since it only occurs once a year. Just as important as it was to tell Jake she cared, it was equally important for Caroline to show Jake through her actions how much he meant to her. Men may not clearly articulate it, but they envision their future wives as considerate and generous individuals. The same holds true for women. They want to be with men who are thoughtful and who dedicate meaningful time to spend together.

Be thoughtful – practice *Ritual 8*.

The geisha prided herself on making people feel happy and taking extra care of them. As your relationship grows, remember that considerate acts are important and show that you truly care. Going out of your way for him contributes positively to your relationship. Thoughtful gestures are an important way to bring two people closer together. In long-term relationships and marriages, demonstrating thoughtfulness is at the cornerstone of maintaining a strong bond.

A first-class geiko is an exquisite willow tree who bends to the service of others.[3]

BE THE PRIZE THAT IS PURSUED

挑 他 的

Exclusive

The geisha understood that her exclusivity made her prized

The mystique of the geisha transcended beyond her iconic beauty as she made herself exclusive to a few select guests. She lived and worked within the private flower and willow world where few were allowed entry and most outsiders could only dream of receiving an invitation. If a man wanted to meet her, he first had to be invited into the society. Money alone could not get him into the *karyukai*. He also needed the right connections. The only way to become a new guest of an *ochaya* was through a personal reference from an existing guest who already had a good standing in the *karyukai*. After a recommendation was made, to be one of the few selected, a recommended guest had to be deemed trustworthy, educated, and well cultured, in addition to being wealthy enough to host an *ozashiki* in an *ochaya*. If a recommended guest was not sure if he could afford an *ozashiki*, then he would not be given the chance to prove it. If there was any doubt, then he could not be a guest of the *karyukai*. The *ochaya* chose their guests. Not the other way around. [1]

Once a guest was accepted and he wanted to meet a geisha, then he could not contact her directly. He had to make arrangements through the office or individual who scheduled her appointments. [2] In the 1960s, a two-hour *ozashiki* with a few guests and three to four geisha in attendance could easily cost more than two thousand dollars. Today, the same *ozashiki* would cost around ten thousand dollars. In Asakusa, a district in Kyoto, the cost of an *ozashiki* was calculated in units of time known as *tamagushi* or flower charge. Translated literally, *tamagushi* means an offering of a sacred spring to a Shinto God. [3] As the evening was meant to feel sacred, no money changed hands on the night of an *ozashiki*. Every detail was considered to make the experience as exclusive as possible for a man who was worthy of the geisha. Having access to the most sought after geisha was a status symbol in Japan.

The geisha was exquisitely beautiful and an accomplished artist, but she was even more alluring because few men had the opportunity to converse with her. To be a guest meant that a man ranked amongst the most powerful, wealthiest and educated in Japan. Men aspired to host an *ozashiki* so that they could live decadently for a moment in the flower and willow world, experiencing all that only the geisha had to offer. The opportunity to have an *ozashiki* was so rare that a guest felt as if he was royalty when entertained by the geisha. This is how you want to be – rare and exclusive – like a gem whose value is equivalent to the most sought after geisha.

Be the prize and conduct yourself accordingly

You are kind and thoughtful, yet approachable and likeable by men. As the geisha was not easily accessible, you should be somewhat unobtainable. Be kind with your words and intentions, but do not reveal yourself completely to a man. By having a positive presence, men will be naturally drawn to your energy. Little words are necessary for a man to notice you. You may have noticed that the woman who is not available is often the woman who is approached by men the most. Or when you have a boyfriend, you tend to get asked out more than when you are single. When a taken woman walks into a room, her presence is not screaming, "I need a man!" Instead, men are saying to themselves that they would like to get to know her better. She possesses validation and desirability. Be a woman who has a positive spirit and a strong inner confidence, without indicating that you are available. A man appeals to a woman's independence coupled with liveliness, which makes a woman more intriguing and attractive.

Manage a man's pursuit of you

Allow a man to uncover you gradually and let there be a mystique about you. It is a man's instinct to pursue a woman and you will lose your allure if you do not allow him to do what is natural. Ask yourself how you let a man get to know you. After a first date, do you call a man or do you wait for him to call you? As a man is getting to know you, are you always available to him? If you have a boyfriend, are you constantly asking if and when he will marry you? Whether it is the initial conversation you have with a man, your first date, or a year into your relationship, you must allow a man to pursue you. Otherwise, he may not be motivated to move forward.

❋ Be nice and partially off limits at the same time. If you give a man a compliment, then allow him to talk and take the lead in the conversation once you make the compliment. Your compliment has signaled to a man that you notice him, but having you is not a given. Your mind and presence should be in a friendly state, but you should not be talking constantly.

❋ Subtly attract a man and gain his interest. There are ways to get a man to take notice of you so that he wants to have a conversation with you. Now that you look your best and are naturally subtly sexy, your actions thereafter will further entice a man to speak to you and ask you on a date. You should not have to ask a man out. He will want to ask you out given that you present yourself the right way.

❋ Show discretion by not making yourself available to every man who is single. The more available you are, the less desirable you seem. Possess a positive, fun spirit while not appearing to be seeking out a man to ask you out on a date. With the combination of your outer and inner beauty, plus your positive mental state and outgoing attitude, men will take notice of you and find ways to speak to you. When this happens, it is up to you to be at ease, while not revealing too much of yourself in the first conversation.

❋ Be relaxed around men. If you are relaxed, then you will appear as if you do not need a man. This may pose to be a challenge to men and they will want to pursue you more. Try not to appear nervous or too eager to impress a man.

- If you see a man that you find attractive, then it is helpful to look in his direction so he can see you notice him, but you should lead your eyes elsewhere so you are not gazing too long at him. You should not be thinking, *"I wish he would ask me out."* Keep yourself occupied with other thoughts because if you are waiting around for him to speak to you, then you are mentally distracted and your demeanor can turn into either nervousness or aggressiveness. A man may sense this so subtly allow a man to pursue you.

- If a man shows interest in you, then have him work a little to get you. Do not make yourself available all of the time. If a man asks you out, then do not tell him your calendar is completely open. A lot of men will lose interest if you appear easy to get. By being independent and having your own life, you are more attractive.

- In the beginning, let him initiate dates. If a man wants to see you every night of the week, then that is his choice. If he is interested, then he will let you know by asking you out regularly. If he is not trying to see you all the time, then he is not really interested.

- Make yourself as desirable as possible. Do not admit you have not been on a date in a while. It is not his business. A man does not need to know about your past dating life. It will not make your relationship better so there is no benefit to bringing it up.

- Maintain some mystery and keep a man intrigued by showing him just a glimpse into your being. Be careful not to reveal too much about yourself. A man does not need to know all of the details of your day and personal life. The less he knows about you in the beginning, the better. If there is some mystery to you, then he will be more intrigued to pursue you.

- Start the first date with a positive attitude and focus on enjoying a few hours out. Avoid setting up expectations beyond that. If a connection is meant to be between the two of you, then it will happen naturally. Approach the date with a relaxed, open attitude. If a connection is not established, then it was a few hours of your life that were necessary to determine whether the man was right for you. It is nothing more and you should not allow it to be anything more. It may be awhile before you meet the *one* with whom you make the right connection. The more comfortable and accepting you are of this fact, the more desirable you are to men because you will appear only obtainable to the *right* man.

- If a man calls you and leaves a message, then do call him back. However, call him only once. Do not leave him multiple messages, send him emails, or text him to make sure he knows you called him back. It is excessive and a turn off. You are no longer a challenge if you are pursuing a man.

- Do not initiate a call to a man. If he does not call, then avoid coming up with excuses that justify why he did not call. If he is not interested, then that is ok. There is someone better who is more worthy of your time and company. If a man is truly interested, then he will be eager to hear your voice.

- Do not track down where a man will be so that you can accidentally run into him. If he is interested, then he should be initiating the effort to see you.

- When you first meet or are getting to know a man, do not appear as if you want a serious relationship. Men shy away from commitment and want to be the one to initiate a relationship. If you communicate to him that you would like to be in a relationship, then it means you are easily obtainable and less of a challenge.

- When you meet a man, do not evaluate him based on how he would be as a husband. Most men can sense when a woman is looking for a husband. Let the man be the aggressor and the one who conducts the chase. The furthest thing from a man's mind is marriage. A man wants to enjoy his time with you in the present and not be the means to an end.

- Do not say that you want to get married. Men think a single woman who wants to get married is a single woman who is desperate to find a husband. You are a prize that a man must earn. You would only marry if a man is worthy.

- Do not cancel plans to see him. If he really likes you, he will suggest another day and find a way to see you. You should not cancel plans until you are in a committed relationship. When a woman bends over backwards for a man from the first day, he never treats her as well as he should.

- Never give him more than a kiss on the first date, and if you do kiss him, make it short. In many areas, it is common for a woman to sleep with a man on the first date. Women have to be careful because when a man is ready for a relationship, there are very few men who will marry a woman they slept with on the first date.

❊ Avoid letting a man see your place until you have been out with him several times and you feel like you know him well. Your home is very personal and says a lot about you. He does not need to see pictures of your family or your bedroom until he is worthy. You have to set limitations. A man should not be invited into your home to enter your personal space until he has earned the right.

❊ If it does not work out with a man, then do not dwell on it. Do not call him. Do not ask him what went wrong. Do not let him see that you are upset. Move on quickly. The more you are exclusive, the more intriguing you are to the *right* man.

❊ When you have a boyfriend, wait for him to be the first to say, "I love you." This is part of the pursuit for a man.

❊ Allow him to be the first one to bring up the subject of marriage. This is also part of the pursuit. If he never brings it up, then he is not ready for it. When a man proposes, he needs to feel like he won a woman over.

❊ If he brings up marriage, then it is appropriate to talk about it and let him know your feelings. It is not appropriate to constantly tell him that you want to get married. A man does not respond well to a woman putting pressure on him to make one of the biggest decisions of his life. If a man really wants to marry a woman, then he will propose faster if his girlfriend does not pressure him into it. Once again, it goes back to a man's need to pursue.

- You do not want a man to feel forced into proposing to you. Never give a man an ultimatum. When your boyfriend asks you to marry him, you want him to do it because he is completely in love with you and he cannot imagine life without you.

Allow a man to follow his natural instinct to pursue a woman

A woman who looks too far in the future misses the present. Stay in the present. Your ability to savor each day will ignite a man's desire to pursue you. When a woman understands this, she holds one of the keys to what drives a man to love her in the long-term. Lisa, who recently celebrated her thirtieth birthday while living in Hong Kong, missed this point in relationships. She could never keep a man around for long because she was determined to get married and made certain to let it known to everyone around her. On the weekends, Lisa would browse through real estate listings online, dreaming of a home for her future family. She clipped pictures from magazines of her ideal engagement ring and dream wedding dress. She even picked out a maid of honor dress for her best friend, Melanie, who lived in Manhattan where Lisa grew up. Melanie found Lisa's obsession with marriage amusing. Melanie, like Lisa's other friends, did not think that Lisa was being unrealistic for believing that it was only a matter of time before she met her future husband. Lisa was beautiful, feminine, smart, kind, and humble. Her girlfriends thought a man would be lucky to be with her. Unfortunately for Lisa, men avoided her as soon as they got to know her because she could not help but bring up her desire to be married and have a family. As with the case with many women, it was natural for Lisa to want this. She even sounded sweet when she talked about having a family, but men did not think so. Whether it is calling you his girlfriend, saying I love you for the first time, or proposing marriage, a man needs to come to it on his own. Lisa's best friend, Melanie, had better luck with men because she approached each date with no visible intentions beyond enjoying her time on the date. Men liked taking Melanie out because she was pretty and had a great personality, but equally as important, there were no future expectations. When Melanie dated Zach, he immediately found himself enamored with Melanie's beauty and light spirit. Melanie shrugged Zach off and never took him seriously when he talked about their future together. She continued to enjoy her dates with Zach and after three months, Zach started refer- ring to Melanie as his girlfriend, unprompted on Melanie's part. Even after Zach's declaration of love, Melanie still took their relationship one day at a time, having fun with Zach and not saying much about their future. After being together for a year, Zach proposed. He told Melanie that he was madly in love with her and could not imagine spending a day of his life without her. Fortunately for Zach, Melanie said yes.

Melanie did not interfere with Zach's intent to pursue her. Instead, she focused on enjoying her time with him in the pres- ent. Zach was left to decide on his own whether Melanie was the one for him. If you let a man be who he is, then he will pursue you if he continues to be intrigued by you. If you pur- sue him, then he is likely to quickly lose interest. If you allow him to pursue you and he does not, then you should move on rather than try to force what is not meant to be. Either way, you must let the man take the lead in determining where the relationship goes.

Be the prize – practice *Ritual 9.*

As the geisha and flower and willow world were mysterious and alluring, there should be exclusiveness about you as well. You arc more desirable if you are not easily obtainable. Men are attracted to the mystery of a woman. There are many aspects and layers that make up your entire being. Reveal them slowly. It is a man's natural instinct to want to win the woman that he finds most attractive. To want something is precious, to be wanted by a man is divine.

No amount of money will buy your way in [the karyukai]. The only key to unlock the door of a Kyoto teahouse is an introduction from a customer, and in Japan introductions are not made lightly. Which means a foreigner could spend years making the necessary connections. And a traveler passing through town doesn't stand a chance.[4]

WAIT TO GIVE YOURSELF TO A MAN

Pure

The geisha's discretion made her highly desired

Contrary to the western depiction of geisha, the *okiya* (houses where geisha lived) were not brothels. The geisha was a professional artist who entertained at *ozashiki* by displaying her superior skills as a dancer and musician. She was among the most accomplished in Japan at performing the tea ceremony and writing calligraphy. Her skills were vast, requiring talent and hard work to achieve her accomplishments. Over the past centuries, brothels and prostitutes have tried to imitate the appearance of the geisha because she was highly desired by men, but the traditional and true *okiya* were off limits to most men. Tradesmen were only allowed to enter the *okiya* in the late morning after most of the inhabitants of the *okiya* had left the house for the day. Tradesmen included the iceman, kimono salesmen, caterers, bill collectors, and others who were greeted in the *genkan* (front entranceway). Typically, there was a bench that they could sit on while conducting business since they were not allowed further entry inside the *okiya*. Male relatives were allowed to enter as far as the dining room. Only priests and children were allowed deeper into the *okiya*, and dressers (most of who were men) were only allowed in the main dressing room. Being a dresser was a highly skilled profession that took years to master, and having a good dresser was critical to the geisha's success. To protect the geisha, no man, no matter who he was, was allowed to come and go as he pleased. [1] If a man was to spend the night at an *okiya*, then the chastity of the geisha who lived there was questionable, which could effect the reputation of the *okiya* and the geisha.

The geisha's reputation held great value. If she did not practice discretion, then she seriously jeopardized her status as a geisha because she represented a symbol of exclusivity. She entertained select guests with her artistic talents and her skills as a master conversationalist. Prior to World War II, the only man she was supposed to have an intimate relationship with was her *danna* (patron) and in many cases she did not. Some geisha even went on to marry their *danna*. After the end of the war, *danna* no longer existed and the geisha was only intimate with a man at her discretion or as part of an enduring relationship. [2]

The men with whom a geisha was intimate mattered as well. Back in 1853, American warships sailed into Edo Bay in Japan demanding a peace treaty and free trade. Three years later, Townsend Harris, America's first consul general arrived, settling near Edo. According to legend, Harris, a heavy fifty-two year old unmarried man, requested companions for himself and his young Dutch assistant. Japanese authorities were not taken aback by the request because within the Japanese culture it was believed access to women was the natural right of men of a certain status. Though, for a senior diplomat, licensed prostitutes, which were legal in Japan, were not good enough. Two young Shimoda geisha, Okichi and Ofuku were coerced to become the diplomat and his assistant's lovers. Initially horrified by the idea, both were eventually persuaded to do it for their country. The relationship between Okichi and Harris was brief and unhappy. Harris abandoned Okichi and her career as a geisha was ruined. No Japanese man would become her patron or guest after she had been with Harris. The rest of Okichi's life was dark and lonely and she was sentimentally remembered as the sacrificial victim for Japan-U.S. relations. From her tragedy was born the legend of Puccini's *Madame Butterfly*.[3]

The geisha had to guard her reputation and practice discretion with whomever she was intimate. Otherwise, she jeopardized her status as a renowned artist. The same holds true for you when you are meeting and attracting men. Your accomplishments and talents may be vast, but a man will be hesitant to build a lasting relationship with you if your intimacy can be easily given away. Your intimacy is one of your greatest treasures. Allow it to be valued as it should be – a prize of riches that you are bestowing on the *right* man.

Be patient and enhance your exclusivity

Building desire creates the greatest culmination to earn the intimacy of a woman. Demonstrate your high value and build excitement. By being exclusive you are signifying to a man that to be with you is to have a special experience. When you are intimate with a man, it should be a bestowed gift that represents a deep connection between two people. Since casual sex is now acceptable for both men and women, then it is easy to make the mistake of sleeping with a man too soon. Most women do it with the intention of showing a man that they care for him. When you sleep with a man without knowing each other well, there is no culmination and a bond is not established that would lead to your intimacy having deeper meaning. To be more appealing and allow the opportunity for a relationship to evolve, you should not easily give up your intimacy.

The geisha proved that a woman is more desirable if she is intimately exclusive. Despite being hard to obtain, the geisha still possessed much sensuality and was sexier because of her exclusiveness. Being sensual should be subtle and complimentary to your other qualities. If you attract a man purely through your sexuality, then he will view you as a woman whose only value is in bed. Instead, draw a man's attention with your intelligence, kindness and other inner qualities, complimented with your subtle sensuality. A man will know that he must wait and win your heart if you are to be intimate with him.

Demonstrate patience and create intrigue

A man is intrigued by the idea that he is one of a few who have been intimate with a woman. To be the most desirable woman, practice making yourself exclusive. How long is it until you are intimate with a man? Do you think it is appropriate to sleep with a man after the first couple of dates or do you make him wait longer? A woman who sleeps with a man quickly creates the impression that she does it with every man. She may hold little appeal for a man beyond spending a few nights with her. If you wait to be intimate with a man, then he will treat you with greater respect and it will be easier for him to view you as a girlfriend or future wife.

❋ When the first date comes to an end, regardless of how well it went, do not go home with a man and do not sleep with him. If you do, then there is a good chance he will not call again. If he does call you again, then he will probably only want to see you for one reason.

❋ If you want a man to view you as a woman that he would be fortunate to marry, then you cannot sleep with him right away. In many cultures there is a double standard. It is acceptable for men to sleep with as many women as they like, but a woman has to appear as if she has slept with no more than a handful of men. Many men are only interested in dating pretty women who will have sex with them. Then one day when they are ready to settle down, they only want to date pretty women who have not been with many men. This is not fair. However, if a woman wants to improve her odds of marrying the man she prefers, then she has to make men wait to gain her intimacy.

❋ A man wants to experience the heightened sensation of gaining a woman's intimacy. If you have sex too soon, then this sensation may not be fully realized. This is unfortunate because it is rare that any of these encounters turn into a lasting relationship.

❋ Never let a man pressure you into having sex. There are too many instances of women giving into the pressure and then never hearing from the man again. Women need to make it more difficult for men to be intimate with them.

❋ Never feel obligated to sleep with a man because he has taken you out for a couple of nice dinners. A man may expect it, but by no means should you play by his rules. Your intimacy cannot be bought.

❋ When it comes to sex, men will push the limits because it is their nature. You have to set limits. If a man is only interested in sex, then let him prey on another woman.

❋ The best way to find out what a man really thinks of you is to wait to be intimate with him. If he sticks around, then you know he cares about you. If he does not, then you know he just wanted to have sex.

❋ When you are finally intimate with him, make it special and be exclusive with him. He does not need to know about your past lovers. It is best to be discrete and unforgettable.

Be cautious of putting liberated sexual views into practice

Your intimacy is one of the greatest gifts you can give to a man. Value and bestow it only on the man who is worthy and has earned the honor of receiving your gift. Kim's modern view on sex proved to be the opposite of this perspective. Kim was a smart, beautiful, easy going, and independent woman in her thirties, living in Los Angeles. She was actively dating with the hope of finding the *one*. She believed that if a woman wanted to have a one-night stand with a man, then she should. Kim's philosophy was that when it comes to sex, women should be as liberated as men. So Kim slept with whom she wanted and when she wanted. If Kim had a good time with a man on a first date, then she would go to bed with him. Unfortunately, she found herself perpetually disappointed because most of the time her date would not call the next day. If he did, then he only stayed around for a few weeks.

Kim came to accept this as normal because she was convinced this was the way men were. At the same time, Kim was depressed because she was hoping one of her dates would turn into a serious relationship, which they never did. She was sure she was having bad luck and that sleeping with men on the first date had nothing to do with whether or not they wanted to be with her over the long-term. After years of this, a friend advised Kim that if she wanted a boyfriend, then she had to stop sleeping with men so quickly. She should make a man wait months. The idea seemed ridiculous to Kim as it challenged her liberal view of women's sexuality. She was certain no man would stick around if he had to wait months for sex, but since she had nothing to lose she decided to give it a try.

A couple of months into her commitment to remain celibate, Kim noticed there were men who would not call her again if she did not go to bed with them by the second date. Kim did not care because most of these men would not have called her back anyway if she had slept with them. To Kim's surprise, she also discovered there were a handful of men who did call after the second date and they did not pressure her to have sex with them. These men were truly interested in getting to know her better. Although these relationships fizzled over time, the longevity of Kim's subsequent relationships increased. Eventually, Kim met Tyler whom she really liked. Though it was hard, she waited to sleep with him. Once they were finally intimate, Tyler continued to pursue her. Their relationship developed into a serious one and they were engaged two years later.

Kim's predicament mirrors many women. They do not understand that when a man sleeps with a woman within the first week that he knows her, it is hard for him to remain interested enough to develop into a relationship. There is nothing left that is physically driving him to her and he is less intrigued. He does not feel the need to get to know her more as he already knows her most intimate, non-exclusive side. Modern society may have an open attitude about sex and it may be more acceptable than ever for a woman to have casual sex. However, if you practice this view, then it will be harder for you to find a long-term relationship. If you wait to give yourself to a man, then he will view you as the sort of woman he may want to marry.

Be patient – practice *Ritual 10.*

From the first date be certain not to expose yourself completely. Let a man gradually get to know you. Allow there to be a build up to each intimate moment. Your intimacy is a gift for which few men are worthy. Be a beautiful mystery that may only be uncovered by one man. Let the *right* man feel that he is worthy by making him wait to be intimate with you.

Relatively few Japanese have ever seen a geisha in the flesh. Even fewer have the considerable financial resources needed to mix with geisha as patrons or regular customers. Fewer still have the background in traditional Japanese arts needed to fully appreciate and enjoy their private performances. And fewest of all break through the glass wall surrounding the flower and willow world.[4]

BE AT EASE
IN ALL YOUR
ENDEAVORS

Peaceful

The geisha exuded calmness

The geisha had a calm presence and made tasks appear effortless. Whether she was leading an intricate tea ceremony or performing a complicated dance, she did so with grace and poise. She appeared as if she was born to do it. The flower and willow world was created as a place of healing and guests entered into a serene atmosphere. Traditional dances were performed to the sound of the *shamisen*, exquisite kimonos were presented, and gentle smiles of the *geiko* and *maiko* lifted the hearts of guests. This culture of healing in the *karyukai* has been refined over hundreds of years. The geisha possessed a unique ability to lift spirits, touching guests simply by her presence.[1]

The geisha offered a place of escape for the elite consisting of Japanese politicians and businessmen. They worked hard in strict environments under high pressure to succeed, so they desired to get away to a place where they could relax. The Japanese believe that as hard as one works, time outside of work should be as pleasurable as possible. Little entertaining happens at home. The world of play is *soto* (outside).[2] *Hanamachi* were designed with this philosophy in mind, to create the ultimate place for relaxation and entertainment. The flower and willow world was a private escape to a decadent, tranquil world of esoteric beauty where the geisha was the center. Men sought her out so that they could experience the exquisite and relaxing environment that she provided. This is how you want to present yourself – beautiful, calm, and at ease. Your presence should be as inviting to a man as the flower and willow world and geisha were. A man should long for your company because of the happiness and tranquility you create when being with him.

Present ease and create a welcoming environment

As you first meet a man and are getting to know him, be at ease. By doing so, you are creating a fertile environment to get to know him better. Your warm presence provides a welcoming platform for a man to converse with you. Men are drawn to and seek out environments that are relaxing. If you appear at ease when you are with a man, then you will present a calm place to which men want to retreat. Stress and tension can turn a man off and strain any relationship whether you have been on three dates or together for two years. The less anxious you are, the happier you will be and your happiness will transfer to those around you – especially men. When a man is around you, he should feel as if he is entering a world that is inviting and warm. It is your kind words and calm attitude that will make him feel good and miss you when you are away.

Not only is it important to create a relaxing environment when you are in the presence of a man, but it is also important for your own well-being. Stress leads to illness and physical problems. It also puts you in a negative mindset and can bring on anxiety and depression. Manage your stress as opposed to allowing it to overwhelm you. Your priority should be to remain at ease so that you can project a positive mindset. Being at ease will enable men to be drawn to you. You are a beautiful woman and your mental state deserves to be treated well just as the rest of you.

Exhibit ease at all times

Try to envision how a person comes across when they are stressed. Do you know men who are high strung? Can you imagine dating a man who is anxious and constantly on edge? If you do not find this quality attractive in a man, then most likely a man will not find it attractive in a woman. Very few men enjoy being around a stressed woman. Most of the time when a woman is high strung, she does not even realize that her anxiousness may sabotage her chances with men.

Take an honest look at yourself and decide if there are aspects of yourself that you need to work on to allow you to be more at ease. Do you easily become stressed? Do you complain a lot? Do you worry too much? Do you easily become upset? If you can answer yes to just one of these, then now is the time to not just cover up the anxiousness, but internally address it. Life is filled with a series of stressful situations. Women say that finding the right person would eliminate their anxiety. Rather than allow stress to dictate your emotions and set your demeanor, recognize these instances and devise a plan to address and resolve them.

✺ Create a routine that helps manage stress, ensuring that you follow through even on days that are especially stressful. Maybe you can take a yoga class or a long walk, or find a peaceful place to clear your head. If stress feels overwhelming, then this is the time for you to take a break and allow your mind and body to relax.

✺ When you find yourself in a stressful situation, then approach it with a peaceful attitude. You will only stress yourself more by being anxious. If you approach stress with a peaceful attitude, then you can turn the moment into one that cannot affect you, resulting in you being more likely to solve your problems with well thought out solutions.

✺ Regardless of how difficult the task, make it appear effortless. Learning how to effortlessly execute may be frustrating at first, but over time you will relish your womanly strength to accomplish anything with intent and grace.

✺ Slow down when you are in overdrive, especially when you are not at work. At work you may have to be aggressive to succeed, but as soon as you leave you should morph into a feminine woman who approaches the world with ease and grace.

✺ Try not to speak loudly and avoid raising your voice. Most people raise their voice when they are anxious or irritated. A loud person is not relaxing to be around and will turn most men off.

✺ Complain rarely. Look for the positive in negative circumstances. The more you complain, the unhappier you will be. Finding constant fault in people and situations will lead to unwanted and unnecessary stress for you. If you complain rarely, then you will be happier and be more attractive to men.

❋ When you entertain, create a relaxing environment. When guests are relaxed, both parties will be happy.

❋ Do not let little things stress you and let go of disagreements. Stress creates anxiety. There are so many little things that can lead to stress if you let them. It is difficult for anyone, including a man, to be around a woman who is always anxious.

❋ Be relaxed. Every time a man is with you, you want him to feel the way that you feel at a spa. The more relaxing you are to be around, the more a man will want to be with you and the more difficult it will be for him to give you up.

❋ Try to be at ease at all times. The geisha had to have the presence of mind to remain calm in the midst of disaster.[3]

❋ Be able to laugh and do not approach life too seriously. The geisha did more than master her art form. She required playful artifice and a sense of humor.[4]

You should appear at ease when making an impression on a man

The way in which you present yourself to a man is directly reflective of how a man believes you will be most of the time. If you appear at ease, then a man will be drawn to your calm, light presence and he will want to spend more time with you. If you appear stressed, then a man may have second thoughts or immediately decide he cannot be with a woman who is anxious and tense a lot. This was the case for Lisa, an expatriate living in Hong Kong. She was constantly stressed about her future and whether she would get married. "If I meet the *one* tomorrow, then how long will it be until our wedding day? Can I wait another two years until I get married? How long do I have to date a guy before I can ask him when he will be ready to propose to me? What happens if I never get married? Will I turn into a spinster?" These were questions that plagued Lisa. Although she mostly bothered her girlfriends with these questions, this anxiety seeped into her interactions with men. They could sense her anxiety when they were around her and quickly lost interest.

It was in Lisa's nature to worry. She worried if she did not make it to the gym four times a week. She worried about men. She worried about being late. She worried about getting promoted at work. Lisa had a successful career because she did worry, but worrying all the time made her unsuccessful with men. Unfortunately, Lisa's anxiety effected her ability to let a man pursue her. She was so worried that if she did not push the relationship forward, then she would never get married. If Lisa were at ease, then she would not have to be preoccupied with marriage and would give a man the opportunity to pursue her.

Lisa's best friend, Melanie, never so much as breathed a word about desiring a boyfriend and ended up engaged to Zach without any pushing on her end. She had the advantage of being at ease. No matter what happened, Melanie never allowed herself to be shaken. When placed in a stressful situation, Melanie would approach her problem with composure and work it out one step at a time. This was one of the reasons that Zach loved Melanie. He liked the idea of spending the rest of his life with a partner who was always collected and calm. Deep down, men desire the same thing as women – a harmonious, peaceful relationship.

Even though Lisa was smart and beautiful, her anxious and stressed demeanor made her less attractive. Similar to Lisa, you may be naturally more emotional than most men, but you must learn how to easily laugh and not be overly tense. If you can manage your emotions and be at ease, then you will be more desirable to be around. Men are sensitive to anxiety and most men try to avoid it. They do not seek it out in a female companion and they do not envision putting themselves in a high-strung environment for the rest of their lives. Men desire a woman who makes them feel relaxed and happy.

Be at ease – practice *Ritual 11*.

Being at ease has a powerful effect when attracting men. It shows a man that you are not only calm, but you are also exhibiting confidence and security. Allow your presence to be light and at ease so that a man is further drawn to uncovering the beauty within you. Having a calm demeanor and a sense of humor are some of the best ways to put your mind in a positive place and attract men to initiate dialogue. You will feel good about yourself and men will be drawn to your presence. A man wants to spend his life in a place that is relaxing and serves as a retreat. By being at ease, you will possess the peaceful atmosphere that men seek out.

A first-class geiko is a master of creating an atmosphere of relaxation and amusement.[5]

SHOW YOUR APPRECIATION

Gratitude

The geisha always showed her appreciation

The geisha understood the value of being grateful to all those who helped her within the flower and willow world. This included the *maiko* and *geiko* whom she called older sisters, the owners of the *okiya* and the *ochaya* whom she called mother and aunts, and the people who lived and worked in the *hanamachi*. The geisha often accompanied the mother of her *okiya* when she visited the people to which the *okiya* owed a great debt. Personal visits to say thank you were paid to the owners of the *ochaya* where the geisha had performed the night before, the dance and music teachers who taught her, the mothers of allied *okiya*, and the local artisans and craftsmen who dressed her. There were many talented and skilled people involved with presenting one geisha.[1] It was especially essential that the geisha paid courtesy calls so that she remained on good terms with the people who helped her. When she graduated from *maiko* to *geiko*, she became financially independent and her *okiya* no longer helped cover her dance and music classes, one-of-a-kind kimonos, and other necessities that completed her as a professional artist. To continue to receive the support of those within her *hanamachi* who helped her, she showed her appreciation by paying personal visits. This informal visiting was how relationships were cultivated and maintained within a *hanamachi* and was critical to its success.[2]

As much as the geisha showed her appreciation to those within her *hanamachi* who helped present her, she was even more appreciative to her guests. Her guests directly and indirectly supported everyone within the *hanamachi*, from the geisha to the *ochaya*, *okiya*, dance and music teachers, the kimono makers, and other artisans and tradesmen within the *hanamachi*. The geisha entertained and served each guest to the best of her ability with the help and support of others in the *hanamachi*. Anyone who was a part of the exclusive and elite flower and willow world – from the guests who cherished the experience of the beauty of the *karyukai* to the other *geiko* and *maiko*, mothers and aunts, craftsmen and tradesmen, teachers and artists – the geisha showed her appreciation to all. Without them, she could not be a geisha. Her appreciation was captured in *The Five Hearts* written for the geisha as a constant reminder of her humility.

The Five Hearts – Geisha House Motto

1. A gentle and obedient heart – to have the heart to say "Yes"
2. An apologetic heart – to say "I'm sorry" and admit and reflect on mistakes
3. A modest heart – to give credit to others for any accomplishments

4. A volunteer heart – to say "I will do it" without thought of benefit
5. An appreciative heart – to say "Thank you"

These thoughts and words should be incorporated into your life. They serve as a guide to showing your appreciation. As the geisha could not be successful without expressing her appreciation, you too must express appreciation if you want to have success in a relationship.

Demonstrate appreciation and create a bond

Showing your appreciation to a man builds a stronger connection. It exhibits the depth and range of your heart. It indicates that you are aware of and sensitive to what a man gives of himself. You are letting a man know that you value him. The geisha appreciated not only the ceremony presented to the guest, but the effort and time that went into creating every detail of the *ozashiki* for the guest. She expressed her appreciation to each individual within the flower and willow world because she valued and respected the core human action of giving of oneself. Following the custom of the flower and willow world, you should show your appreciation to the people who help you and give to you the most. This especially applies to the man in your life.

Showing your appreciation to a man will result in a kind gesture being returned. It is natural to give more of oneself if it is appreciated. When you give of yourself and the receiver expresses how appreciative he or she is, then you are more likely to give to that person again. A relationship with a man is the same way. If a man feels appreciated, then he is likely to love you more and give more of himself in return.

Frequently show your appreciation

Every day there are moments when you can express your appreciation. A few words go a long way. Do you always say thank you? Do you recognize a man's thoughtful gestures? When he does something extra thoughtful, do you express that you are grateful? Showing your appreciation should become second nature to you. Whether you are on your first date or on a date with your boyfriend of two years, you should always be appreciative. It shows you value him.

❉ Always say thank you when he does something nice for you. Even when you have a serious boyfriend, it should not be assumed. To keep a relationship strong each person should value the other.

❉ Be grateful for every nice thing he does, including the little things. No matter how simple and small, you should always show your appreciation.

❉ If he does something thoughtful and it is not exactly how you would go about doing it or what you wanted, then appreciate the effort he made. Substance matters more than appearance. If he surprises you with tulips and you wanted roses, then appreciate that he bought you flowers. Your attentiveness to him will enhance his attentiveness to you.

❉ Every time he takes you out for dinner or spends a Saturday afternoon with you, he is choosing to spend his time with you and money on you over anyone else. Have realistic expectations and be appreciative of his affection.

✿ One of the best ways to show your appreciation is to do something thoughtful to show that you are thankful for the nice things that he does for you.

Be humbly appreciative of all that you receive

It is good to set high expectations for yourself and not settle for less, but you should always be grateful for all that you receive whether it is a gift or success in life. Eva, was accustomed to having her way with men because she was beautiful, smart, and sexy. She was in her late thirties living in London and was never short of boyfriends. Men would put her on a pedestal, going out of their way for her so much that she came to expect it. Ordinarily, it did not matter if she was unappreciative, but it was not helping her situation with her current boyfriend who she hoped would become her husband. It was not a surprise that Eva loved Justin because he was many women's ideal man. He could have almost any woman he wanted.

Justin was brilliant, handsome, and wildly successful. He took Eva out every night to the best restaurants, whisking her away for the weekend on exotic vacations, and lavishing her with gifts. Justin willingly did these things for Eva because he adored her. As time passed, he began to notice that Eva rarely showed signs of gratitude. He even dropped hints on several occasions, alluding to the nice things that he had done for her. Eva ignored his hints. Justin felt that Eva's inability to be appreciative this early in the relationship was a sign of what was to come if he were to marry her. He had seen it too many times with his married friends. They had wives who expected their husbands' time, money, and emotional presence, while showing little or no appreciation in return. After being together for six months, Justin did not see any signs that Eva would change so he broke up with her. In Justin's eyes, Eva was spoiled and did not understand what it meant to value him and all that he had given to her. He wanted to treat Eva well, but he also wanted Eva to be grateful for his thoughtful gestures. Eva, on the other hand, did not understand how important it was to show Justin, a self-made man, that she appreciated him.

Everyone wants to be appreciated. The more a man gives of himself, the more important it is that he feels appreciated. Most men give a lot from the first date to being in a committed relationship. A man will continue to want to spend time with you if you genuinely value him. He wants to be appreciated for what he brings to the relationship just as he should appreciate you.

Be appreciative – practice *Ritual 12.*

You must never forget to show your appreciation. Just as you worked hard to become accomplished and uniquely beautiful, a man worked hard so he could treat you well. Always be conscious and grateful of what he does for you. Possessing the ability to naturally express your appreciation is a quality a man desires in a lifelong companion.

Gift giving is a deeply rooted part of Japanese life, an important way of maintaining good relations with friends and colleagues.[3]

RITUAL **13**

BE COMPASSIONATE

Compassion

The geisha's compassion was healing to men

Possessing the ability to exhibit compassion was quintessential for the geisha to connect with her guests. She exhibited compassion by providing a man with a private romantic world where he was free from the pressures of the outside world. Most of a Japanese man's time was spent at work in an environment with strict rules to conform and succeed within a predefined mold. Japanese society was rigid and all members had their appointed roles. There was no place for individual expression. Even at home, marriages were arranged and wives were expected to raise the children and take care of the house while the man focused on his work. It was not uncommon for a man to feel very emotionally connected to a geisha. She may have spent years getting to know him personally, becoming a close friend.

The geisha understood that men wanted a refuge that contrasted with their daily responsibilities. When a man entered an *ozashiki*, he left the stress of his daily life behind and entered the flower and willow world where he was greeted with the geisha's soft voice and kind smile welcoming him. She was there to listen to him and relieve him of stress, even if it was only for a few hours. The geisha was his confidante. He was free to express any emotion or thought and it remained between him and her. She possessed the ability to heal with her compassion.

As the geisha could heal a man, you should know how to express compassion and be supportive of a man when he needs it. Open your heart and allow yourself to feel others' emotions so you can read when a man is bothered. The geisha was especially sensitive to the feelings of others. She believed that she had to learn how to feel and read her guests' emotions so that she could connect with them on a very personal level. A Kyoto guest who happened to be a musician conferred with the geisha to help him find depth to his music. "My music expresses deep feelings about love between men and women, so I must use geisha for inspiration – they are more affectionate than normal people." [1] Men were drawn to the geisha because she showed more compassion than ordinary women. Your ability to be sensitive to a man's feelings will draw a man closer to you and he will turn to you as a confidante.

Show compassion and deepen your connection

Even if a man is emotionally guarded, you should still show you care. Men are prone to bottle up their feelings, appearing to be indifferent. Part of it is biological and part of it is sociological. For women it is more natural and acceptable to show their emotions, which is why men often turn to a woman when they are seeking compassion. A man likes to lean on a

woman for support because her voice and touch are soothing. She can easily show sympathy and compassion and can
provide thoughtful wisdom. Though with more women being
independent and taking on roles that traditionally belonged
to men, some women have lost their soft touch and repress
their natural tendency to be sympathetic. Yet, compassion is
a quality men admire and desire in a woman.

Recognize moments when you can be compassionate,
whether they are with your boyfriend, one of your close girlfriends, or a family member. There are times when others are
in need of an appreciative or compassionate heart. Everyone
wants to feel that someone cares about his or her well-being.
By expressing compassion, you are showing that you have a
true caring heart and you can touch a man in a way that few
can or do.

Exhibit compassion

To gauge whether you are being as compassionate as you
are capable of, ask yourself how do you react to a man when
he desires sympathy. Do you notice when a man wants you
to show that you care? Do you refrain from saying something
or do you try to help him feel better? Do you think it is best
to block feelings in emotional situations? With the demands
of life and the need to survive as an independent woman,
many women believe there is not a reason to be compassionate. Some women put up walls to prevent people from taking
advantage of or hurting them. Other women are tough on
men because they are tough on themselves. But the ability
to show compassion is a wonderful quality and one that men
desire in women. Allow yourself to feel a man's emotions. Be
conscious of how you express emotions and know when to
show compassion to a man.

❧ Be supportive of a man in both the good and bad times. There will always be those instances when one does not want to deal with the bad times. Whether it is a financial hardship or an illness, plenty of women (and men) only want to be around for the good times. A man wants a woman who will be by his side for both the good and bad. If you spend the rest of your life with someone, then inevitably there will be bad times.

❧ If he is going through a hard time, whether it is his job situation, a family issue, or another problem, show him that you care. When a man is going through a stressful stage, he may appear unemotional. However, do not assume that this means that you should be indifferent to his feelings. Always show concern when he is upset.

❧ When he is upset, show your compassion by listening to him and helping him work through his challenges (if he asks for help). You do not need to have all of the answers to his problems. What is important is that you listen and show that you care.

❧ A man does not expect you to be tough. He wants to be with a woman who is sympathetic and sensitive.

Be career driven, but do not lose your ability to show compassion

In today's work world, compassion is a quality that has little to no influence on most people's career success. Yet, it is at the cornerstone of strengthening a relationship with a man. This was the challenge that Keri faced, which she did not fully understand. Keri was thirty-five and living and working in New York City. She prided herself on being competitive and was determined to become a partner at her law firm. To do so, she had to be tough and driven as there was only one female partner at her firm. Keri was admirably determined and worked hard, but she was unable to differentiate her drive at work from her relationships with men. She lived her life, both at work and personally, with a stern and unrelenting attitude. Her boyfriend, Tim, took on a similar persona at his job as a successful trader at a top investment bank. Keri thought that they made the perfect couple. As far as she was concerned, her life could only be better if she was married to Tim.

Almost a year had passed since Keri had met Tim and she was certain a ring and proposal would follow in no time. Their one-year anniversary arrived and Keri waited for the big surprise from Tim. He had told her that he wanted to stay in for the evening to talk to her. Keri was convinced that this was the night that Tim would propose. She spent hours getting ready, dimmed the lights in her apartment, filled the rooms with candles, and put a bottle of champagne in the refrigerator. After all, they would have to celebrate right away.

When Tim arrived at her apartment, to Keri's surprise, he had a concerned look on his face. Before Tim said a word, Keri knew what was coming. As Keri suspected, Tim proceeded to break up with her. He claimed that for the year that they had been together, Keri was self-absorbed, oblivious, and living in a bubble. He cited all of the times that she was insensitive and how the relationship was primarily about making her feel good. Whenever he had a problem, she told him he needed to be stronger and ignored him. He said that the relationship had to come to an end because he had realized in the last month that he was no longer in love with her.

Angry and shocked, Keri turned to her best friend, Cindy, for comfort. She relayed to Cindy what Tim had said to her. When Keri asked Cindy if she was insensitive like Tim had claimed, Cindy was silent. Keri repeated the question and

Cindy stumbled over her words, trying to explain that Keri was not the most sympathetic person. Keri defended herself, called Tim weak, and declared that she would find a better man who was not as needy as Tim.

What Keri could not see was that it was not fair of her to criticize or ignore Tim when he was seeking compassion and support from her. Like Keri, too many women do not realize the importance of or know how to be sympathetic and attentive to a man when he wants or needs emotional support. Compassion is not a quality you need to be a successful, independent woman. It matters more that a woman is resilient, motivated, focused, and ambitious. In some cases, if you are too soft, it may work against you in the professional world. However, when it comes to men, they desire a woman who can exhibit compassion.

Be compassionate – practice *Ritual 13.*

It is natural for a man to desire a compassionate woman. Everyone wants someone in their life who will console them. When life is at its toughest and a man just wants to feel good after a hard day, compassion is the quality he will appreciate most in a companion. What matters to a man is your ability to listen and understand. It means opening your heart to his feelings of distress so that you can better comprehend his feelings. It means knowing how to say the right words that will make him feel better. It means that your presence as a true and trusted friend will comfort him most. Within every woman lies the ability to heal a man. By possessing the ability to heal through compassion you will touch a man in ways that few others can.

A person who can feel the joy of something beautiful and the pain of something sad is almost like a mind reader – she is capable of sharing happiness and hurt, she knows what to say and how to say it, and she can repair wounded hearts. The best maiko all have this ability.'

BE DELIBERATE IN YOUR COMMUNICATION

Wisdom

The geisha thoughtfully communicated her ideas

The geisha was careful not to offend or upset others and thought before she spoke so that she could express herself appropriately. As she entertained powerful people from all over the world, she was a de facto diplomat who had to communicate well with anyone – expressing her thoughts and opinions without offending. This does not mean that she was passive. She was sharp-witted and insightful when she entertained powerful people from all parts of society and from around the world.[1] By using the right words and having a poised demeanor, she gracefully communicated her ideas while remaining respectful of others.

As important, the geisha spoke thoughtfully to all of those within the community of her *hanamachi* – *maiko* and *geiko*, Mothers, owners of the *ochaya*, teachers, artisans, tradesmen, and anyone else who was a part of the flower and willow world.

Many of those living within a *hanamachi*, geisha included,
spent most, if not all, of their lives there. *Hanamachi* were insu-
lar, private communities in which relationships within them
lasted many years, and in some cases, a lifetime. Harmony was
prized above any other social value. Characteristic of Japanese
society, a peaceful coexistence mattered most. This was even
more pronounced within the flower and willow world in comparison to the rest of Japan. The flower and willow world could
not succeed unless everyone worked together and got along
with each other.[2] To be a geisha meant that she must know
how to express her thoughts and opinions without causing
offense to others. This was key for her to earn the support
and friendship of both guests and members of the *hanamachi*,
which were instrumental to her becoming a success.

Just as the geisha was admired and liked because she communicated well, you want to be poised and intelligent when
you are expressing your opinions. Communication is essential
to all relationships, whether it is a relationship with someone
who have known for a longtime or someone who you are first
meeting. Your words represent you and the better you communicate, the better you present yourself. A man's attraction
is influenced by the tone you use to speak, the words you
choose, and the intent behind your words. Your purpose and
emotions are revealed clearly through your voice. Be mindful
of creating constructive communication.

Men will respect and admire you more if you speak thoughtfully

Women are naturally more expressive and emotional
than men, which can be both wonderful and challenging for
a woman. It is good that a woman can easily show a man how
much she cares. However, just as a woman may passionately
care about a man, she may become equally angry when upset.

You must know how to articulate well and choose your words wisely when you are frustrated. It is best to find a balance in the middle and keep your emotions under control. If you blow up and scream, it is hard for anyone to take you seriously or comprehend what you are trying to communicate. If you are upset for legitimate reasons, then talk through the problems. A man will be receptive and more likely to work with you to resolve the issues.

A man is attracted to a woman who is thoughtful when she speaks. Being able to gracefully handle a disagreement shows strength and maturity. You are exhibiting intelligence through clear and smart communication. The ability to turn a disagreement into a mere conversation using calm words is a wonderful skill to master. A woman who speaks thoughtfully, in a calm manner when faced with confrontation, is subtly sexy to a man. Being steadfast in resolving conflicts, while being inoffensive and respectful to others, is a true talent.

Demonstrate thoughtfulness and wisdom when you speak

Examine yourself and determine how you react when you are placed in a confrontational situation. When you become upset, do you explode? Do you say things you later regret? Must you have the last word in an argument? At times, you may want to demonstrate that you are an independent thinker. However, realize that you can do this by choosing your words wisely. These are not mutually exclusive. It is important to show discretion. In all conversations, be respectful of what others say and thoughtful in your speech.

❀ When you are upset, take a deep breath and think before you speak. Focus on being calm so that you can articulate your feelings intelligently.

❋ Try to keep your emotions under control. A man would rather spend time with a woman who is positive and rarely whines or yells than with a woman who screams and has constant meltdowns.

❋ If you are tired, do not argue. Take up the conversation at another time. When you discuss a disagreement at a later time, you both are in a better mood and it is more likely to be a conversation rather than an argument.

❋ Do not be passive, but at the same time, pick your battles carefully. It is not about winning, it is about living in harmony. There are women who are ultra-competitive and have to win every argument with everyone. A man does not like it when a woman has to be right all of the time, just as a woman does not like it when a man must always be right.

❋ When you speak, choose your words wisely. A man may act tough on the outside, but a man does not want to be the recipient of harsh words doled out by the woman in his life.

❋ The less emotional and angry you appear, the better you will communicate. The geisha always appeared in control of her emotions.

❋ Gauge the tone of your voice. Forceful, loud sounds can be construed as anger when in a disagreement. A soft, melodic voice is composed and soothing. You should appear poised when you are engaging in a dis-agreement. Your words should calm any aggression expressed by both parties. Your voice has the ability to win a man over.

It is good to have an opinion, but be thoughtful when you express it

Men admire a woman who has her own beliefs and is an individual. Even though a woman is independent she should be aware of others, demonstrating consideration and respectfulness. Maria struggled with this and said whatever was on her mind, unknowingly offending men. Now in her forties living in San Francisco, Maria had spent her life saying whatever was on her mind. Her girlfriends found her bluntness amusing, but Maria was not aware that a man did not want to hear that he made a bad choice or did something wrong. When she told a date that the hotel he had picked for his vacation was not nice, he did not want to see her again. Even if it was not a great hotel, she did not understand the impact of her saying so. Regardless of Maria's prettiness or intelligence, a man did not want to be told he was wrong or did not know what he was doing.

You do not have to agree with everything a man says, just as you do not have to agree with everything your friends say. With your friends, you probably censor your opinions because you never want to hurt them and certainly want to remain good friends. The same holds true for a man. If you want to keep a man close to you, then you have to communicate with him in a thoughtful and respectful manner. A man may appear to let a harsh comment not bother him, but you have to be careful because he will remember it even if he does not say so. A man can be especially sensitive because, even though he may not express emotions, he does have an ego and criticism diminishes it.

A different challenge some women have relates to their emotions swinging from one extreme to another. Maria's friend, Lily, who also lived in San Francisco, made a conscious effort to be considerate and thoughtful. She was never short of boyfriends because she was beautiful and had a caring disposition. She was also passionate, which men found attractive. When she was happy, men were drawn to her because she was full of energy and excitement about life. On the other hand, there was another side to Lily's personality. As loving as she was when she was happy, she was just as passionately angry when she was mad. It was impossible to reason with Lily when she became upset. She was irrational and prone to meltdowns. Boyfriends found it hard to be in a relationship with her and often moved on after witnessing a few of her intense meltdowns. Similar to Lily, you do not want to be overly emotional. At the same time, you do not want to be critical like Maria. It is important to find a balance. Be in touch with your feelings, but be able to express them with grace and poise. From the tone of your voice to your choice of words, these can all soften your opinion so that you are able to express yourself in a manner that does not offend others.

Be deliberate – practice *Ritual 14*

Anytime you are upset with a man or disagree with what he says, choose your words wisely and be thoughtful and respectful. Speak to a man as you would like a man to speak to you. It will be hard for him to really hear you if you are confrontational or too emotional. Your independent thought is sexy to a man when it is executed in a soft, feminine manner. A man admires the beauty in a woman's voice whether she is laughing, speaking thoughtfully, or calming a disagreement.

A proper geiko always remains calm, no matter what happens.[3]

BE ATTENTIVE AT KEY MOMENTS

Considerate

The geisha attracted men with her attentiveness

Every moment that the geisha was with a guest, she paid extra attention to each detail so that the experience was exquisite. When a guest entered an *ozashiki*, all in attendance administered formal bows. The guest of honor was seated in the position of respect with his back to the alcove, which displayed a flawlessly painted scroll or an elegant flower arrangement. The geisha positioned herself at the elbow of the guest, speaking softly, smiling, pouring sake, and presenting little delicacies. At some point in the evening, *geiko* and *maiko* preformed a perfectly executed dance. Special attention was focused on the guest of honor. All was done so that each guest felt unique and tended to in a manner that he had never experienced elsewhere.

To be attentive, the geisha was aware of the guest's desires and sensitive to the guest's needs. Her attentiveness and attention to detail created an environment of harmony and tranquility. This was exhibited when the geisha performed the tea ceremony. The tea ceremony (way of tea) embodies four elements – harmony, respect, purity and tranquility. A geisha prepared extensively for performing the tea ceremony, training for years. Every aspect was to be perfect, yet appearing simple in every detail. Before guests entered the tea ceremony, they walked across a path of clean stones in the *roji* (tea garden), symbolizing ridding themselves of the dust in the world. Next, the guests washed their hands and mouth from water in a *tsukubai* (stone basin) as a final purifying step. The guests entered the tea ceremony through a low door, requiring them to bow. Bowing symbolized that the ego should be left outside and that the back should bend rather than break. The geisha was then ready to lead the tea ceremony.

The tea ceremony was divided into three parts. First, the windows in the room were covered and the scroll was replaced with a new one, often containing Buddhist writings. Tea was served thicker than the usual green tea so that the mind was focused on the moment. Second, a simple meal was served while guests relaxed in the inner garden to reflect. In the final part of the tea ceremony (*nochiseki*), the atmosphere was changed to a bright room and the scroll in the alcove was replaced with a floral arrangement. The geisha performed the *nochiseki* in silence, serving thin tea. The experience of the tea ceremony was a purifying, spiritual release for the guests.

As exhibited in the tea ceremony and reflective of Zen Buddhism, as well as in Japanese culture, the focus is not the end result, but the journey itself. The geisha practiced every aspect of her craft with seriousness and awareness. When she was being attentive to her guests, she was taking care of them in the best possible way, while building a bond with them.

Guests felt a connection to her with each gesture that she made, whether it was leading them through the detailed tea ceremony or performing their favorite dance. It was her actions and presence at that moment that mattered. The loyalty she earned and strong relationships she developed were a direct result of the full attentiveness she devoted to her guests. When you are attentive at the right times, you are paving the path to a strong relationship. As the geisha demonstrated, attentiveness is more important than achieving the goal of creating a relationship. Your focus should be on the path, not the end. The relationship will come if you are aware and attentive along the way.

Be present and the relationship will develop

When you are hoping to be in a relationship, it is important not to focus on the idea of having the relationship as it may prevent you from being fully present in the moment. Instead, your focus should be on how to develop a strong relationship during the key moments that the two of you are together. It is the process or rather, the journey, that matters most. Being aware and fully present is how you should be at each moment that you are with a man, whether you are talking to a man for the first time or you are years into a relationship. It is about carefully listening to what he says and responding thoughtfully. It is about making the most of the moment rather than thinking about the future. It is about making the present time enjoyable and harmonious. It is about having a spirit for today that makes you shine and stand out.

You must realize that being attentive does not mean that you call a man constantly or be at his beckon call. With all relationships there is balance. Constantly showing your attention to a man in every possible way can be overwhelming and smothering to a man. It also puts the relationship out of balance and a woman loses appeal. A woman is more attractive and sexy if she is independent, and understands the right and important moments for her to be fully attentive to a man. For the geisha, this was the few hours of the *ozashiki* where she paid attention to every detail to honor her guest. The rest of her day was mostly spent perfecting her skills so that she could be an accomplished artist. The same should hold true for you. At the times you are with a man and the focus is on the two of you – whether it is a date or you are relaxing together at home – this is when it is important to be extra attentive.

By being attentive, you are also differentiating yourself. When you are attentive and it is genuine, you are enhancing your beauty. This applies to whether you are performing a thoughtful act or you are passionately engaged in conversation. A man is drawn to a woman who is mentally present and cares to put her full attention towards her gestures. As you listen to a man, similar to the geisha, your face should have a genuine smile so that he knows that you are listening and encouraging him to speak. You are open to his ideas while being supportive. When you allow yourself to talk about a topic of which you are not knowledgeable, you are showing resourcefulness. You are being helpful even without being asked. It is your instinct to give to the man in your life because he is important to you. This is what it means to be truly attentive.

Demonstrate attentiveness

What are the steps that you can take to be more aware and attentive? Do you carefully listen to a man and truly absorb the depth of what he is saying? Do you show you are supportive when something is important to him? Are you willing to compromise at times even if you feel that it is not necessary, indicating that you are open to his ideas? Do you make him feel good about himself? Do you let him know when you think he has a good idea? Following how the geisha was fully present when she was attentive to her guests, if you do the same for the man in your life, then he will long for your company.

❋ Always be mentally present when you are spending time together. This applies to whether you are on a date with your boyfriend of a year or on a first date. When particularly on a first date, it is a turn off to a man when a woman is mostly focused on talking about her issues or rambling on about subjects that only interest her. It is important to allow a man to make a connection with you on a first date. It is not the right place to vent about work or personal problems. The same holds true for when you are in a relationship. The special time you set aside for each other should feel special. A man should walk away feeling intrigued and energized about the time spent with you. This is what makes a woman exciting on a first date, as well as after being together for five years.

❋ Relationships are give and take. Make sure you give as much as you take. Giving means that you are attentive to him, whether it is offering to help him do something or making sure that you always listen to what he says. It is natural to want to pay the most attention to what personally interests you. Rather than choose what you want to respond to, be attentive and aware of all aspects of him. This is how you will fully connect with a man and is an important element in building a long-term relationship.

❋ When you are in a relationship, make time for the man in your life by making him feel wanted. The longer you are with a man, the easier it is to get in the habit of putting him second. There will always be issues with work, family, or other obligations that keep you busy. No matter how much you having going on, remain attentive to him. A man wants to feel that he is needed by the woman in his life. Couples who put each other first have the most successful relationships.

❋ Be open and flexible. To be fully attentive means that you are an active listener. It is good to have your own opinion, but allow it to be his time. Your opinions and actions should be open and flexible. There are times when he should do the same for you, but allow there to be moments when you give your undivided attention to him. When you do this, you are showing him that you support and care about him.

You can be independent and attentive without compromising your modern values

Being attentive and yielding to a man's desires at times may be counterintuitive to being independent, but when practiced correctly, the two ideas will complement one another. Lucy, a woman in her forties living in London, discovered that this concept helped her with relationships with men. Lucy ran her own business and treated the men she dated in the same manner in which she ran her company. It was her nature to be tough and in control. If she was not, then her business would not be successful. She never compromised in business or otherwise, which was beneficial when applied to the right things. Unfortunately, this was the same approach that Lucy took with men. She wanted to be with a man who always agreed with her and put her needs first. If Lucy wanted a man to treat her well, then she had to be attentive to him, just as he would be to her. It took Lucy quite a while to figure this out, but after years of trial and error she finally did. As a result, she found that she was more successful with men.

When Lucy began being more open, she discovered that she did not always have the right answer as she had previously thought. She also found that the men she liked were more interested in her if she showed interest in their ideas and was respectful when they shared them with her. Men especially liked attention from her because they valued her opinion since she was intelligent and successful at business. When Lucy gave men room to be themselves and listened and responded thoughtfully to them, she discovered that she also felt good because men were finally appreciating her the way she wanted to be appreciated – for her wisdom and intelligence. Lucy realized that it was much easier to be attentive than she had formerly imagined and the end result was that men found her more attractive. Lucy's former image of being attentive to a man was cooking him dinner every night and giving him a massage. She was not comfortable doing either of these because they were not an accurate reflection of herself.

When Lucy started dating someone seriously, she figured out that there were other ways to tend to her boyfriend that worked well without comprising her modern values. Lucy's new boyfriend wanted to go skiing for their vacation while Lucy wanted to relax on a beach. She told her boyfriend that she would be happy to ski, but for the next vacation she asked if they could go on a vacation to a beach. He easily agreed. During their ski trip, Lucy even surprised him with a massage at the hotel spa. She had subtly attended to him at the right moment and she was as happy as him.

Lucy decided to retain the same attitude with her boyfriend even after their vacation. If she did not agree with him, then she did not insist on being right. She realized she did not miss being argumentative. She found that in a relationship, it was not important to her to feel as though she was constantly in control like when at work. She also found that she really enjoyed taking care of her boyfriend. In return, her boyfriend respected and supported her ideas and needs. Since she had a more positive mindset, then it benefited her relationship, her well-being, and her business. Lucy was encouraged. All aspects of her life were thriving as she had what mattered most to her – a boyfriend with whom she was happy. Ten years prior, Lucy would have refused to give a man special attention because she believed she would be giving up her independence. What she did not realize was that this was a key element to a relationship, and it actually resulted in making her life more fulfilled. By giving her full attention to her boyfriend, she helped create a harmonious relationship and hopefully a long-term future together.

Be attentive – practice *Ritual 15*.

Being attentive is the journey that will lead to a strong relationship with a man. It is your presence of mind and attention to detail that will make each moment special and memorable to him. Your caring nature will shine through and he will see the beauty in your soul. He will want to be with you because your extra touch brings him a joy he rarely experiences.

Along with her artistic accomplishments, the geisha is also master of the arts of making her customers laugh, stroking their egos and keeping their glasses topped up. [1]

DEEPLY CONNECT TO A MAN

Understanding

The geisha understood how to connect to men

The geisha possessed an acute perception of men and their needs. She connected with her guests the moment she entered the *ozashiki*. Prior to the *ozashiki*, she would research the guest of honor and make certain that she could speak of the guest's interests. Her research included knowledge of relevant politics and current events. If her guest were a politician, then she would study the legislation that he was sponsoring. If he were an actor, then she would read articles about him. If he were a singer, then she would listen to his music. If he were a writer, then she would read his writings. If the guest were a foreigner, then she would study aspects about his country. The geisha spent much of her time in bookstores, libraries, and museums researching her guests to best understand their accomplishments, interests, and areas of expertise. This was a key phase in establishing a connection with a guest.

She further understood her guest by observing the *ozashiki* from the moment she entered. Every *ozashiki* was different, even within the same *ochaya*. The arrangement of the room revealed the status of the guest of honor. From the value of the scroll hanging on the *tokonoma* to the choice of dishes on the table and where the food was from, the geisha would modulate her behavior accordingly. Each guest was catered to individually as the geisha tailored the conversation and entertainment to the guest's preference. She knew what her guest of honor most enjoyed – watching a dance, engaging in witty conversation, or perhaps playing amusing games. Over time, as she spent more time with her guest of honor, the geisha committed to memory his personal likes and dislikes so that each experience at the *ochaya* was personalized.[1]

The geisha's superior hosting provided to her guests extended beyond offering the best in entertainment that Japan had to offer. *Ochaya* were also used for sensitive business and political discussions. An *ozashiki* provided a secluded environment where a guest knew his privacy would be protected. The geisha entertained some of Japan's most recognized politicians and businessmen. She witnessed the making of major business deals, government policy, military strategies, and assassination plots. In the nineteenth century, the geisha also served as a protector to her guests. Her hair ornaments were originally designed with pointed ends so that she could defend her powerful guests from attack. Her coral hair ornaments were used to test the safety of the sake because coral breaks apart when it comes in contact with poison. Sometimes she would position herself near the entrance to a room and let the guest of honor know when someone was approaching by making a discrete signal. She would inform anyone who approached that the guests did not want to be disturbed. The geisha understood that there were times a man wanted a secluded, private environment and she took it upon herself to provide it.[2]

By understanding her guests, the geisha formed strong bonds with men. She became a confidante and close friend. Guests could discuss arts and business with her, yet also trust her with the most secretive matters. Getting to know and understand a man better than others in his life enables you to create a personal connection that is unique to being with you. He will turn to you because he trusts you and that you understand him as others cannot. Being understood is essential for a strong relationship. It is one of the qualities a man values most in a female companion.

Understand the male ego and he will be drawn to you

When first meeting a man, you should make an effort to understand him. This will benefit both of you. You will benefit because you will know sooner, rather than later, whether or not you like and connect with him. He will benefit because he will be impressed that you are taking the time to understand him, fostering an immediate connection to you. When you are with a man, ask questions and listen with interest and attention. That way you are discovering more about him, but at the same time, you show that you care to know more about him.

When being in a relationship with a man, understanding him will strengthen your bond and bring you closer together. By being able to understand how he feels, what he thinks, and what his passions are, you are reading into his personality and knowing him in a way that most others do not. From family to friends and co-workers, a man can be surrounded by others who do not truly understand. Throughout your relationship, if you make an effort to connect to a man more personally than others, then he will feel a bond with you for the rest of his life.

Strong bonds happen only in the rare instances when two people connect with each other in a way that they do not with others. This is with the relationship with a best friend. You immediately feel a connection and become close friends. However, there are also rare individuals who possess the ability to know everyone well. Others are drawn to these few individuals because others feel understood upon shortly interacting with them. The geisha was one of these rare individuals who said and did the right things so that she understood her guests well, whether they had met once or had known each other for years. Like the geisha, you can be the woman who every man you meet feels a connection.

Know how to understand a man

When a man talks about himself or something that interests him, listen and ask insightful questions. There is so much to learn about a man if you take the time to ask the right questions and demonstrate understanding. Other than knowing where a man grew up or the kind of car he drives, what else do you know about him? Do you know what lies underneath his surface – his interests, goals, and hopes? How well do you know each man you have dated? If you are on a first date, then be open so that you can understand your date as much as possible. If you have a boyfriend, then always be interested in his life and continue to understand him as he grows and evolves. As you are not the same person you were ten years ago, he is not the same as he was when you first got to know him.

* What are his interests and hobbies? Listen and let him tell you as much about himself as he is willing to tell.

* Do you know what he does at his job? Do you know what he believes is the ideal work situation? A man's

identity is a reflection of his view of work. If you understand his view of work, then you will understand him.

❋ What drives him in life? Is he highly competitive? Does he want to be respected in his field? Does he like his work or does he want to retire as soon as possible? What are his life goals and what would he like to achieve? What drives a man will tell you a lot about his ambitions and hopes.

❋ What is he passionate about? Is it sports? Does he love to travel? Is he a wine collector? What is most important to him? If you know what he is passionate about, then you know how to reach him.

❋ What makes him happy? A good meal? Being successful at work? Going on vacation? Playing a sport? Being with friends? For a geisha's guest, an *ozashiki* was the opportunity to enjoy the very best in Japanese cuisine, relaxation, conversation, and refined entertainment.[3] What does he enjoy?

❋ Who does he admire and why? His boss? His parents? A writer? A musician? Someone famous? Someone who is accomplished in his field? If you know whom he admires, then you know whom he would like to strive to be. You also will understand the qualities that he values the most.

❋ What inspires him in life – music, art, writing, his work, being outdoors, a person, a place? If a man connects to music, then ask him why. If he is happiest outdoors, then understand why. His answers will reveal so much about what moves him emotionally.

You will connect to a man better if you know how to reach him

A woman who easily connects with others also easily gains men's attention and interest. Cindy was one of these rare women. She would step back, remove the attention from herself, listen and observe, and allow a man to be himself so that he could reveal his desires and beliefs. Unlike her friend, Keri, who was uncompassionate to her boyfriend, Cindy, always showed that she cared and was interested in what a man had to say. By peeling back the layers of a man, Cindy could quickly figure out what was important to him. If he mentioned a family member in a positive way, then he was probably close to his family. If he spoke fondly about a senior colleague in his field of work, then he admired or wanted to be like this person. There was so much Cindy learned about men just by initiating and engaging in conversation with them.

By showing men that she was interested in what they had to say, men felt that Cindy understood them. When a man would talk about his job, Cindy would encourage him to do so. She understood men talk about work because it is a significant part of their identity. For this reason, it is even more important to listen and ask questions. A man may be opening up and letting you be privy to some of his most significant desires and feelings. Do not tune him out – this is when it matters most that you show that you are interested.

Both men and women sought Cindy out for conversation and sympathy because she always seemed to understand. When a man had a meaningful conversation with Cindy, he would walk away feeling good and connected to her. This is how you want a man to feel about you. Whether it is on your first date with someone new or the boyfriend that you have been with for a year, you should know a man as well as possible. If you ask questions, understand his ideas and goals, and express that you relate to him, then he will feel a stronger connection to you.

Deeply connect to a man – practice *Ritual 16.*

To understand a man is to know him. Just as you are a mystery to be uncovered, a man is a puzzle that you must piece together to fully see. By knowing him, you will reach him in a way that other women cannot. At the heart of every successful relationship is the intersection of interests, passions, wants, goals and dreams. The attention you give to getting to know a man bridges the gaps through your demonstration of being understanding, providing comfort, and developing a sense of familiarity. Every man wants to be understood and respected for his beliefs and passions. The woman who understands him better than anyone else is the woman he wants to know for the rest of his life.

What is said and done in the privacy of an ozashiki may be divorced from reality of the outside world, but the relationships that develop within are very real.[4]

ALLOW A MAN TO EMBRACE HIS MALENESS

Respect

The geisha made men feel empowered

Men went to great lengths to be the guest of the geisha for a mere few hours because in the geisha's presence a man felt elation no other woman could replicate. The geisha symbolized luxury, romance, and exclusivity to the wealthiest and most powerful men of Japan and the world. She was a rare work of art as she embodied beauty and possessed great artistic talent. To know her was to be in the company of a woman with undisputed class and consummate artistic achievement. To be her patron was to be able to afford her sumptuous kimono and elegant surroundings. To be able to converse with her and please her was to be *iki* (chic). To understand the symbolism of her dance and the words of her songs was to be a connoisseur.[1]

Having access to a geisha was equivalent to belonging to an elite men's club. Only the wealthiest and most powerful men could gain entry. Men competed with each other to support the most popular geisha, and the more prominent the geisha, the higher the status symbol in Japanese society.[2] The geisha was the ultimate trophy for men and everything she represented tended to the male ego. She set the stage for a man to feel important. The guest of honor was the center and he felt privileged to have the opportunity to know her. As a man defined himself as a connoisseur for understanding the depth of the art of the geisha, the geisha defined herself by her art. Like the geisha, your inner beauty defines you. Create the opportunity for a man to be proud to have won your love and to have you by his side.

The geisha was the exquisite art admired by all in attendance, while the man was the guest of honor at the *ozashiki*. Both were leaders, but in different ways. You must recognize that men are different from women. Each should receive equal attention in a relationship, but attention should be provided in a different manner for each partner so that the two do not combat one another. You should always be conscious of this equal balance. If the relationship goes out of balance, then it will be difficult for a man to be in the relationship. Your value is your beautiful feminine ways, vast accomplishments, witty conversation, depth of intelligence, kind intentions, thoughtful gestures, and ability to heal by your voice and presence. As important is your ability to embrace his spirit and ideas and treat him as if he is your guest of honor. The right smile and acknowledgement from you will make him feel important. In doing so, he will continue to turn to you so that he can experience that feeling again and again.

Connect with the male ego and you will understand a man

Understanding a man and encouraging him to be himself also means that you are allowing a man to embrace his maleness. Men are testosterone- and ego-driven and want to be with a woman who respects their maleness, allowing them to be themselves. As you know, a man prefers a feminine woman rather than the mirror image of himself. Since women are more independent than ever, then it is easy to forget about the male ego. There must be a distinction between the two of you – you are the woman and he is the man. You can still remain self-sufficient in your own ideas while at the same time letting him feel like a man. What makes you unique is that you embrace your femininity while remaining strong and independent at the same time.

There are times when you will lead and there are times when he will lead. The goal is to live in harmony and understand when it is important to let him lead so that he feels empowered. The geisha allowed few men entry into the flower and willow world. Just by allowing a man to feel he had exclusive entry, he felt important. Like the geisha, making yourself appear exclusive enables a man to feel as though he has succeeded in winning your love. By allowing him entry into your world, you have led the relationship. You have tapped into your feminine beauty and are empowered as a desirable woman who knows she has great worth.

The geisha was one of Japan's most revered performers. Men felt it was an honor to watch her dance or listen to her play music. Men sought out her conversation because she was witty and well read. At these moments, the geisha enabled men to feel empowered by having the honor to be in her presence. There will be times when you have a brilliant idea or solution and a man will admire you for your ideas. He will recognize that you are an independent woman and he will know that you can take care of yourself. These traits make you especially attractive. What a man does not like is for a woman to feel as though she has all of the brilliant ideas and his opinion does not matter. A man is attracted to a woman who compliments him and makes him feel good about his ideas and beliefs. In return, he admires and praises her for her independence, intelligence, and accomplishments. A woman is sexy when she recognizes her independence and that she does not necessarily need a man, yet she chooses to be with a man because she feels her life is better with him.

Know how to allow a man to feel like a man

Ask yourself what your specific role is in a relationship and what it means to let a man embrace his maleness. Are you respectful of a man's opinions? Do you demonstrate that you are supportive of his ideas? A man wants to be with a woman who makes him feel as though his opinion is important. As he admires your vast beauty and accomplishments, you should respect his successes and appreciate his ability to take charge and make thoughtful decisions.

�֍ Let him know that he is important. A man wants a woman to appreciate him. It is a man's natural instinct to feel needed, whether it is at work or in his personal life.

✳ Treat him with respect. A man wants to be respected by others, but especially by the woman in his life.

✳ If he does something that impresses you, then compliment him. A man wants to feel appreciated and who better to do so than the woman in his life.

❋ Convey to him that his opinion matters to you. Be respectful of his thoughts and do not diminish his ideas. The more open you are to his ideas, the better you will get along with one another. In return, he should be supportive of your ideas as well.

❋ Be careful not to degrade him about his job or career. Most of a man's identity comes from his work and the ability to succeed. Be supportive of his career, especially when he is at a crossroads and trying to improve his job situation.

❋ If you disagree with him or he does something you do not like, then do not let him know while in the company of others. Wait until you can speak privately and then bring up the subject politely. Talk about it in a non-confrontational manner. It is embarrassing for a man when the woman he loves puts him down in front of others, especially among his family and friends.

❋ Be faithful and loyal to him. A man wants to be with a woman who is faithful and loyal to him in all situations. Even regarding something as simple as a small dispute, you should be careful about complaining to others about him. As a significant and influential person in your life, he should be treated with the utmost respect.

❋ Encourage him to be a wonderful lover. A man equates his masculinity to his ability to perform in intimate situations.

❋ Allow him to feel like he is a leader at the right times. If you make a big decision that concerns him, then be humble about it and let him feel like he was a part of making the decision.

Promote balance and equality in a relationship

In every relationship there needs to be a balance between the male and female. Finding this balance is one of the biggest challenges men and women face, whether on a first date or after years into a relationship. Keri struggled with finding a balance in her personal relationships as at work, men continuously surrounded her at her law firm. In her pursuit to become one of the only female partners, she adapted the traits of her male colleagues. Unfortunately, her dominating personality extended to her relationship with her boyfriend thereby adding to the reasons for Tim breaking up with her. Besides being uncompassionate, Tim felt that Keri put him down too much and dominated the relationship. If Keri did not agree with Tim's opinion, then she would adamantly disagree as a way to show strength and ensure that her voice was heard. It was typical for Keri to criticize Tim in front of his friends, which drove Tim crazy. Keri also believed that as Tim's girlfriend, she should advise him on his career, especially if they were going to be married one day. Since she had a successful career, then she was certain she knew what was best for him.

Unfortunately for Keri, she did not understand that Tim needed to feel empowered as a man. Tim felt the complete opposite when he was with her. Keri's reaction was that she thought Tim was acting immature by breaking up with her over his views that she was uncompassionate and too controlling. For Keri, these were positive qualities that made her a strong woman. Keri conveyed Tim's accusations to her friend, Cindy, who understood exactly to what Tim was referring. Cindy had observed on many occasions instances where Keri insisted on having her way with her boyfriends. With Tim, she constantly questioned his opinions and decisions and was not conscious of emasculating him in front of his friends.

It was not Keri's role to be Tim's parent or boss. Tim needed to feel like he could take care of himself and be in charge at times. This is why men aspire to run their own businesses, be a partner at the company where they work, or to be leaders in their field. There are many more men who are interested in making it to the top of their field than women because it is a man's instinct to lead. If you understand this, then you understand that a man does not feel complete in a relationship unless he is allowed to embrace his maleness. It is not fair for anyone to always have his or her way or the last word. As a woman, if you do this to a man, then he will feel inadequate. He takes care of you and is attentive to your needs, so recognize his great qualities and respect and admire him as well.

Support a man – practice *Ritual 17.*

Allow the man in your life to embrace his maleness. It is a man's instinct to feel like a protector and a leader – the two places he has the opportunity to do so is at work and in a relationship. If you accept and respect his masculinity, then he will love you more because you fulfill his need to feel important. You have the ability to make him feel better than anyone else can.

She [the geisha] has studied the male ego and tends it like a garden. She knows a man's moods and his seasons. She fusses, and he blooms.[3]

BE AN INDEPENDENT WOMAN

Independence

The geisha captured men's hearts because she was an independent woman

The geisha was considered one of the first modern women in Japan and possessed an independence and freedom that other women of her time did not have. If a geisha was skilled and sought out as an artist, then she had a means of obtaining financial stability. When she was older, she could continue to support herself by being a professional dancer or musician, teacher, or a head of an *okiya* or an *ochaya*. Unlike other Japanese women, in the flower and willow world, women had the command and there was not a stigma attached to being single when older. It also was not considered inappropriate for a woman to be a single mother, which even in modern day Japan is rare and shunned.[1] Few women in Japan had the opportunity to gain the independence a geisha could. The famous geisha, Mineko Iwasaki, earned about $500,000 a year in 1960s Japan, which was more than most presidents of companies. She also pointed out that with earning that much income, the notion that geisha performed sexual favors for her guests was ridiculous.[2]

Unlike other Japanese women, the geisha was given the resources to be independent. The women who worked within the *hanamachi* were some of the most successful business-women in Japan. From the *maiko* and *geiko* and the Mother of the *okiya* to the owner of the *ochaya* and dancers and musicians who taught the geisha, women held the most significant positions within the *hanamachi*. They created the exquisite experience for the distinguished guest. The men within the *hanamachi* held positions as artists, tradesmen, dressers and accountants, but their roles were limited in comparison to the women. Even if a geisha chose to leave the *hanamachi*, the skills she learned could earn her a living elsewhere, in the arts or the business sector.

The geisha started her career living and training in an *okiya*. She followed a rigorous regiment of constant classes and rehearsal, similar to the intensity of a prima ballerina, concert pianist or opera singer. The Mother of the *okiya* financially supported her in her efforts to become a professional and later helped manage her career when she debuted. The geisha lived in the *okiya* for a contracted period of time during which she repaid the *okiya* for its investment. Then she became independent and moved out on her own while maintaining a relationship with her sponsoring *okiya*. The exception being a geisha who had been designated as an *atotori* (an heir to the *okiya* and successor). She carried the last name of the *okiya* through birth or adoption and lived in the *okiya* throughout her career.[3]

During her training, the geisha became educated, acquired an art and skill, earned her own money, established an independent identity, and pursued a romance if she liked. Most Japanese women did not work and had arranged marriages where they were confined to the home. The geisha carved out a niche for herself within Japan, creating the highly desirable flower and willow world. Within this world, men were made to feel like kings by the geisha while she maintained independence that did not exist elsewhere. It was her independent qualities that allowed her to give more of herself and made her more desirable to men. If you are accomplished and independent, you are also resourceful and creative. A man will be drawn to your independent nature in which you demonstrate strength and confidence. He will prefer to be with you because of what you give of yourself to a man is more robust than the average woman. As the geisha's independent qualities captured men's hearts, it is your independence balanced with your femininity and attentiveness that will attract a man.

Create intrigue through your independence

As the ideal female companion, you are attentive and allow the man in your life to feel like a man. However, you must also simultaneously remain an independent woman. Never give up your identity for a man. Allowing a man to dominate a relationship is not intriguing. You are admired because you have your own interests and are capable of taking care of yourself. In a relationship, you should recognize and acknowledge his accomplishments and the importance of his life, but realize your life is important as well. As the geisha did, you must find a balance where you are attentive to the man in your life while continuing to develop and grow your mind and skills. A man falls in love with your identity. Remember that you must always have one that remains independent from a man.

Keeping true to your identity can be hard for many women as they become wrapped up in a relationship. For many women, being married and having children is the top priority in their life. This is when a woman can become most confused about her identity. Do not allow your boyfriend, husband, or children to solely define you. You need to be defined as an independent person. When you have a family, you should be loving and attentive to your husband and children, but realize that your children will grow up and need you less and your husband does not want to have a mother as a wife. This is why it is important that you always remain accomplished in your own. Many Japanese men preferred spending their time at an *ozashiki* over being with their wives. The geisha was a well-educated, revered artist. She was exquisitely classy throughout her life and well into her older years as both a mother and wife. Even at eighty years of age, a geisha had the skills to work as a teacher, mother of an *okiya*, or owner of an *ochaya*.

Embody independence

When you master tending to the man in your life while remaining independent, you are proving that you are the ideal female companion who can switch from being a thoughtful and attentive companion to a decisive and intelligent woman. When you are with him, it is about your relationship. Be kind and doting and eager to listen to him talk about his day or whatever is on his mind. He will like that you are compassionate, humble, and giving. You will further impress him by being self-sufficient, intelligent, and accomplished. Your independence does not create a power struggle. Instead, it lifts the relationship and strengthens it. You have as much to bring to the conversations and the times you spend together as he does. When you are focusing on developing your skills and accomplishments, your life will mainly be about you – whether you are working hard on your career, playing a sport, or enjoying your favorite hobby. You have a life that is separate and defines you – this is your art. What will you do to ensure that your art is always progressing and helping you become more beautiful with age?

❋ Continue to be accomplished. Part of why he fell in love with you is because you are more than a pretty face. Have substance behind your beauty. Over time, you will age. It is your inner beauty that will make you stand out and matter more than your outer beauty.

❋ Be yourself – an independent, strong woman. Just because you are attentive to a man and open to his ideas does not mean that you should let him dominate you. You still have your own ideas and opinions. What sets you apart is that you respect other opinions and are able to communicate your ideas without offense.

❋ When you have a boyfriend, take care of him, but do not center your entire life around him. Many women focus all of their attention on their boyfriends, forgetting about their careers, friends, and family. Remain the woman who won his heart and do not give up your identity. If you are at his beck and call, then you can appear overbearing and less interesting to be with in the long-term.

❋ Be careful about allowing yourself to become financially dependent on a man. If you stop working, then make sure you have a line of work or venture that you can return to if necessary. You never know what will happen in the future. Some men gradually lose respect for a woman when he makes all the money and she stays at home. Too often, a man leaves his wife because he finds another woman he finds more intriguing. Remember that your accomplishments build your self-confidence and make you more desirable. A man will have less in common with you over time if you have little interests or skills. The geisha was admired throughout her lifetime because of her refined art and skills.

❋ Always maintain your own identity. Take care of the man in your life, but do not live through him. If you do so, then you risk him becoming bored with you. Guests of the flower and willow world sought out the company of the geisha because she was interesting, accomplished, and talented. Some geisha even went on to marry their guests.

Why a woman must keep her identity

From the beginning of a relationship and for all of the years that follow, focus as much on developing and growing yourself as you do on the relationship. Both are equally important in order to maintain a strong relationship with a man. Many women do not realize that much of a man's long-term interest in a woman lies in her skills, accomplishments, and independence. Helen had challenges understanding this balance. Helen, in her early thirties and living in New York City's Chelsea district, worked in public relations for a high-end fashion company. She was stylish and hip and did everything right to get a man's attention. Needless to say, Helen was never short of dates or boyfriends. She made a great girlfriend. She was attentive to her boyfriends, telling them they were amazing, and cooking them a homemade dinner every weekend that rivaled the best restaurants in her neighborhood. These were just a few of the thoughtful things Helen did for the men in her life.

Since Helen treated men so well, she became serious with only a couple of men as they were together for years. All of them stayed with her for as long as they could, that is, until Helen broke up with them because they would not propose marriage. Helen's boyfriends, on the other hand, did not feel they were in love with her enough to commit to being with her for a lifetime. Helen gave up most of her life and identity for her boyfriends. If her boyfriend asked her what she wanted for dinner, her answer was, "Whatever you want." She also dropped her friends and family when she was in a relationship. Her life became about her boyfriend and she spent every minute she could with him when she was not working. Helen's philosophy was that if she gave her all to her boyfriend, then it would make for a perfect relationship.

With each boyfriend, Helen fell into the same pattern. As soon as he started calling her his girlfriend, she became less interested in her career and hobbies and she spent less time with her family and friends. She would obsess over her boyfriend, constantly catering to him and trying to push the relationship forward. Rather than garnering a positive reaction, Helen came across as suffocating and less appealing as a future wife. After a year of being in a relationship, Helen would start pressuring her boyfriend to propose. Her boyfriends needed to come to marriage on their own, which they never did. As a result, Helen ended up breaking up with them. It was easy for Helen to gain the attention of a man, but as time passed, she could never get a relationship to grow into a more meaningful, long-term commitment because she would lose her identity in the relationship. She was far different from the sexy, savvy, independent woman that men first met.

When Helen was single, she was accomplished, interesting, and fun to be around. She focused on work and having good times with her friends. At night, she would go to the hippest restaurants and clubs. On the weekends, she would frequent the flea markets for antique jewelry or spend an afternoon at the art galleries near her apartment. When she was working, she was focused on her successful career. This was the woman who won men's hearts. But as soon as a man became a boyfriend, Helen gave up her interests and independence and her career was no longer important to her. Men liked Helen because she took exceptional care of them, but she became dull and clingy. She never wanted to be alone and complained if her boyfriend did anything without her. Helen had lost her intrigue and at times, was overbearing. Boyfriends had fallen in love with the single Helen because she was the ideal female companion, but who they ended up with was someone different.

No matter how much you take care of a man, be sure not to let your personality become vacant because your relationship will become flat. To remain exciting, you must be an independent spirit while being attentive to the man in your life. As tempting as it may be to focus most of your energy on your relationship, over time, you will feel empty and the relationship will be missing a key piece.

Be independent – practice *Ritual 18.*

Live through yourself, not a man. Some women work so hard to please a man that they get lost in the man or the relationship. Other women define themselves through a man, and without the man, they do not have an identity. Know who you are and possess your own identity. In a relationship, two individuals come together to share their lives. It is not only about the man. What you contribute to the relationship equally matters and is just as exciting. A man loves and admires you because you are accomplished and intelligent *and* because you make him feel amazing.

She (the geisha) has studied dance until the movements are second nature, the shamisen (a three-stringed musical instrument) has become an extension of herself. Her training in drums, kouta (geisha songs), tea ceremony and calligraphy will continue throughout her life – she will never achieve the perfection she seeks. But for all her artistic accomplishments, it is her skill in conversation that Japanese men claim to appreciate the most. She has become fluent in the news of the day, the gossip of the theater or sumo world, the naughty jokes making the rounds, and flattery both refined and outrageous. [4]

BE A
DYNAMIC
HOSTESS

Hospitable

The geisha was an unparalleled hostess

The geisha took all of her superior skills and qualities of becoming the ideal female companion and she channeled them into being an excellent hostess. Putting her artistic talents into practice at the *ozashiki* was what she had been working towards since her first day as a *maiko*. The geisha attentively served each guest in a series of endlessly practiced movements and acted as a catalyst to present guests with the most refined entertainment Japan had to offer.[1]

The *ozashiki* were essentially unchanged since the mid-eighteenth century[2] and usually took place in an *ochaya*. The mood was set at the *ochaya* to offer guests an exquisite experience without a single detail being overlooked. The *ochaya* was designed to meet the discriminating standards of customers from the top ranks of Japanese and international society. The aesthetics were derived from the traditional Japanese tea ceremony, embodying the best of traditional Japanese architecture and interior design. The *ozashiki* lasted a few hours in a pristine, private space. Each room had a *tatami* floor and an alcove with the appropriate monthly hanging scroll and an exquisite flower arrangement, which were changed and personalized for each guest to make the experience more special. Cuisine, conversation, and entertainment were also chosen based on the preferences and status of the guest of honor.

At some point in the evening, the *geiko* performed for the guests. The *tachikata* was the main dance performer, while the *jikata* served as an accompanist to the *tachikata*, playing the *shamisen* and singing. Watching the top *tachikata* and *jikata* perform at an *ozashiki* was equivalent to the guest of honor having a private performance in his own home by the most accomplished artists and musicians in Japan.[3] Detailed attention and the goal of perfection was dedicated to every element of the *ozashiki* from where the fan was placed in the tea ceremony to the intricate pattern of an *obi* and the arch of a geisha's eyebrow. The *ozashiki* customized for the guest of honor exhibited that every notion of the flower and willow world was dedicated to beauty so that the guest's experience was enhanced.[4]

The geisha was the trendsetter for fashion, popular culture, and the arts in Japan. She initiated trends that were followed by almost every woman in Japan, including the way of wrapping a kimono or tying an *obi*, the styling of hair, and the leading of a conversation. She was viewed as chic and avant-garde, popularized in the press, romantic novels, and wood-block prints.[5] As the geisha was admired by women and desired by men, you want to make an impression as a superior hostess. The geisha created an environment where guests could laugh, socialize, conduct business, find privacy, relax, or escape from the pressures of everyday life. She intelligently conversed and understood her guests, demonstrating attentiveness to them. She danced, sang, played music at a professional level, and flawlessly performed an intricate tea ceremony. The few men who were permitted in the *ochaya* had an experience that was unique to any other in the world. Being with you should be the same. A man should feel as if he is the guest of honor, never wanting to leave because it is a privilege to be with you.

Be an excellent hostess and create memorable experiences

The better you are as a hostess, the more desirable you are to a man. The skills of an excellent hostess are the same qualities a man desires in a lifelong companion. Creating a beautiful party means that you will present yourself and your home beautifully. Leading and initiating interesting and amusing conversation means that he will always enjoy talking to you and will never be bored. Showcasing your ability to serve guests thoughtfully means you will be thoughtful to him and treat him well. Bringing guests together and organizing a gathering executed with attention to detail means that you are capable of great achievement. Whether it is work, home, or the demands of life, you have the ability to accomplish tasks with ease. Watching you as a hostess, a man will translate your talents into your ability to be a good partner and companion.

As a hostess, you are inviting guests to see a personal side of you and experience the best that you have to offer. You will tailor your gathering to your own tastes with your guests in mind so that everyone has an enjoyable and memorable time. A man will leave with memories that will entice him to want to return and be in your presence again. For a few hours he will escape to a beautiful place where he is free to be himself and encouraged to let go of the pressures and stress of life. He is honored to be the guest of an exquisite woman and he will long to come back so that he may re-experience the feeling of happiness and excitement that your presence brings.

Demonstrate superior hosting

The way in which you host is a direct reflection of your personality and skills. Are you gracious? Do you create a clean environment that is also relaxing? Do you make an effort to look your best? Do men want to spend time with you because you offer engaging conversation? Do you converse thoughtfully with your guests? Are you humble and a good listener? Do you treat everyone equally? Are you at ease? How do you present your home when you host others? Is it inviting and fun? By creating an inviting environment, you make each guest feel wonderful and welcome.

❊ Keep your home tidy and clean. Whether it is your home or attire, you should always appear put together and well groomed. A woman is less attractive as a hostess if her home is messy or she looks like she has been cleaning the house all day.

❊ Be able to put together a meal, whether it is a romantic meal for two or a sit down dinner for ten. You do not have to be an expert chef. Feel free to use shortcuts. It is most important for you to execute meals smoothly. What matters most is that the guests do not wait too long to eat and that the experience is memorable.

❊ Keep at least a few quality wines (both red and white) in your home to serve to guests when they come over unprompted. There are plenty of quality wines you can buy that are inexpensive. If you do not know what to buy, then ask for help at a local reputable wine store. Wine has unique meaning from the type of grape and the part of the world it was harvested to the year it was bottled. These attributes symbolize how the elements of the earth can come together to create a divine drink to be enjoyed and savored. Your unique beauty can bring the same to a relationship and draw a man into the experience.

❋ Always serve food on china, even takeout. Avoid placing food out for guests in takeout containers. Put the food in bowls and accompany it with serving spoons. Paper plates and plastic utensils should be reserved for children and outdoor events. They also are not good for the environment.

❋ Always give guests silverware, whether it is sterling silver, stainless steel, or some other type of metal. Only use plastic utensils when you are eating outdoors or your guests are children. Even for a formal dinner outdoors, you should not use plastic. A good alternative is casual china and inexpensive flatware. It is no longer an elegant dinner if you use plastic and paper.

❋ Use linen napkins and table cloths for dinner parties and more formal occasions. Never give guests paper towels. If you have to use paper napkins, buy nice ones – traditional white or an elegant pattern. Cloth and linen napkins are preferable because they are a nice touch and better for the environment.

❋ Serve guests drinks in glassware. If you like to use a plastic cup when you are alone, then that is fine. However, do not serve a drink to a guest in a plastic cup. Plastic cups are ideal for children and the outdoors. Also, wine should be in wine glasses, not water glasses. If you want to make clean up easy, then you can buy stemless wine glasses that can go in the dishwasher. Keep a decanter on hand for the occasion when a guest brings over a bottle of wine that is worthy of decanting. It is an elegant personal touch and shows the guest that you appreciate his or her gift.

❋ Always offer a few different types of drinks to your guests. You never know when someone will stop by. In your kitchen, keep good tea and high quality coffee (both decaffeinated and caffeinated) on hand. If you make coffee, then trying making it in a French Press. It is easy to do and always impresses people. Also keep on hand milk and sugar, bottled water (both sparkling and distilled), and a few bottles of soda (try something different such as a local root beer). The extra effort highlights your attention to detail and your familiarity with excellence.

❋ Always have quality snacks on hand to serve, such as nuts (they keep for a longtime), olives (they keep for a while, too), crackers, and cheese that will not expire quickly. A man will be impressed if you have a stocked kitchen. He will also be touched if he is served quality food and drink.

❋ If you do not know how to cook, then try to learn. You do not have to be a gourmand. You can focus on quick and easy, delicious meals. There are many dishes that you can make that are simple, yet will impress a man. Sitting down to a homemade meal and sharing a wonderful bottle of wine with a man is incredibly romantic. Your skills as a hostess coupled with your beauty, intelligence, and graciousness will win his admiration.

❈ If you are throwing a party, then be certain to invite guests who are diverse and interesting and have enough food and drinks to serve them. Your choice of music and an extra touch of flowers will add ambience and make a difference. At an *ozashiki*, the ideal guest was refined and well educated. He enjoyed the music and dancing and appreciated the exquisite kimono and *tokonoma* with its seasonal flower arrangement and matching scroll of calligraphy. He understood how all aspects of the room, including the performance, harmonized with the season.[6]

❈ Being a good hostess requires practice. The more often you entertain, the better a hostess you will be. As the famous geisha Mineko Iwasaki said, "Dance and other art forms can be taught, but how to make an ozashiki sparkle cannot. This is something that takes a certain aptitude and years of experience."[7]

What sort of hostess will you be?

As a hostess, you have the opportunity to demonstrate the skills and qualities that you have been perfecting. While you prepare to host, you are preparing yourself to be the woman who wins men's hearts. The manner and way in which you present yourself and your gathering will be how others will perceive and remember you. Melanie, who was living in New York City, made an excellent hostess. She had a relaxed demeanor and attentive personality. Whether she was having a friend over for a drink or hosting a party, she made everyone feel welcome. She created a relaxed atmosphere and her warm voice and kind words encouraged guests to be themselves. To add to the experience, she made sure to serve delicious food and guest's wine glasses were never empty. She also set her table with china and silverware, accentuated with a floral centerpiece. Regardless of the formality of the place setting, guests always enjoyed themselves. Being in a neat, elegant home enabled guests to feel welcome and comfortable. This was one of the reasons Melanie's husband, Zach, fell in love with her. Melanie made guests feel so comfortable and satisfied that Zach never wanted to leave. A man likes to have a scrumptious meal placed in front of him with his girlfriend serving his favorite drink to him in a lovely setting. It is ideal for him, complete with his ideal female companion by his side. Like Melanie, you want to be that hostess for which a man falls instantly.

Just as your guests and the man in your life enjoy them-selves, you want to do so as well. Enjoying your party will make you a better hostess. If you are uptight and overstressed, then the stress will transfer to your guests. Whereas nobody wanted to pass on an invitation to Melanie's dinner parties, Sam could rarely get anyone to accept hers, especially men. Sam would bark orders to whoever passed through her front door. Sam felt that if she was nice enough to offer up her home to host, then guests should help out. Sam was notorious for serving very little food. She was so particular about how she kept her apartment that guests felt uncomfortable in her home. There were too many rules pertaining to what guests were asked not to do, resulting in both men and women not want-ing to go over to Sam's home. Watching how Sam presented herself in her home, men felt that she would be the same way in a relationship.

Being an excellent hostess is dependent on your attitude, demeanor, and skills. The geisha trained for years to become the ultimate hostess – studying dance and music; practicing the intricate tea ceremony; learning the art of conversation; and mastering how to be witty, decisive, amusing, and attentive all at once. These are just a few of the carefully developed skills that the geisha showcased as a hostess. For you, embodying elegance, being intelligent and skilled at conversation, presenting yourself humbly, approaching a man with kindness, performing thoughtful acts, being at ease and compassionate, showing your appreciation, and understanding a man, are all traits that will help you be an excellent hostess. These traits are at the heart of what it means to be a superior hostess.

Be a dynamic hostess – practice *Ritual 19.*

As an excellent hostess you lift spirits and make people happy. Your voice floats across the room like a sweet song as you converse with your guests. Your laughter and words are light and uplifting. You whisk delicacies before your guests, encouraging them to enjoy as you ensure every glass is full. Your demeanor is at ease and your beauty exquisite, like the gathering you are hosting. Where you are, others will want to be. You have created the ultimate companionship for a man.

In essence, this is what geisha do: they entertain people. They are the crème de la crème of Japanese entertainers. Their clients are drawn mainly from the top of Japan's many hierarchies...the ideal guest takes pleasure in the atmosphere of iki (an aesthetic of sophisticated partying associated with the flower and willow world).[8]

KEEP A
MAN
INTRIGUED

Love

The geisha has held up to the test of time

The geisha won the hearts of men as far back as the 18th century. She was the first woman in Japan to entertain through her art. She performed at a professional level and engaged in witty and intelligent conversation with guests. She was the perfect combination of femininity and beauty, each feature of her subtly accentuated, transforming her into a striking and memorable image. She tended to her guests in a way that was unique to the flower and willow world where beauty was celebrated and a few elite guests were shown the best in Japanese dance, music, cuisine, presentation, and aesthetics. She was revered, admired, and loved by men. The world she created was mystical, romantic, and exquisite. She was the ideal companion; the ultimate trophy for a man.

To this day, men are still fascinated by her. The geisha is the international symbol of Japan, yet most Japanese have never seen her.[1] Imposters have posed as a geisha for foreign tourists, but without an invitation to the flower and willow world, the sight of a true geisha is rare. Foreign tourists have gone as far as breaking into teahouses and gardens in the city of Kyoto in hopes of having a glimpse of the geisha within the *karyukai*.[2] Unlike any other group of women, the geisha has become synonymous with attentiveness, elegance, femininity, beauty, and exclusivity. The geisha embodied what men desire. She has always held the secret to winning a man's heart. As your life moves forward, it is up to you to reflect on the geisha and be reminded of her mystique that has captured men's hearts for centuries. In doing so, you will find the way to be forever desirable.

Practice *The Rituals* and you will become the most desirable woman

By embodying *The Rituals*, you will gain romantic independence in the same manner in which becoming a *geiko* enabled the geisha to gain her own independence. When you transform into the ideal female companion, men will naturally be attracted to you. You will place yourself in a position where you have options. If you do not feel that a man is completely right for you, then you do not have to feel pressured to be in a relationship with him. Standing out as the ideal woman means that when you meet the right man, he will desire to be solely with you. As the geisha created options for herself that resulted in gaining more freedom than most other women of her time, you can also create the same path for yourself.

When the time comes for you to meet the right man and make a strong connection with him, you will welcome it. He will prefer to date you as opposed to others because he will find your qualities unique and intriguing. He will feel a special spark with you and it is this spark that will continue to make him desire you. As time passes, it is important to keep this spark alive because without it, your relationship risks becoming flat. If you continue to cultivate and tend to your inner and outer beauty as the geisha did, then with age and time, a man's passion for you will grow deeper and he will fall further in love with you. The geisha understood how to keep a man intrigued for a lifetime. She refined and improved each detail of her being, becoming more desirable with each year. By embodying *The Rituals*, you will grow towards becoming the best woman you can be. You will possess the qualities that will forever make you admired and desired by men – offering yourself as a uniquely beautiful and irreplaceable being.

Keep a Man Intrigued

Geisha from the elite *hanamachi* never stopped training.[3] The same should hold true for you. Everyday you should work to improve and refine your inner and outer beauty. It will not only establish you as the ideal female companion, it will also turn you into a stronger and better woman. Ask yourself if you are embodying all of *The Rituals* and how you can improve on them. Are you as interesting and accomplished as you were when he first met you? Are you attentive at the right moments, while remaining independent? Do you make a point to be kind, thoughtful, and humble in all aspects of your life? Are you accentuating your feminine attributes? Are you tending to your health so that your body feels its best both physically and mentally? Do you continue to be well read and worldly? A geisha could not remain a geisha unless she continued to perfect her skills and talents. She was committed to performing her best in every aspect of her craft, even *wajutsu* (the art of trivial conversation).[4] As the geisha became more desirable with time, you should create the same path for yourself so that when you meet the right man he will remain as in love with you as the first day you intrigued him. By reflecting on *The Geisha Secret* you will understand how to be the woman who is forever desired.

Ritual 1 Make Yourself Uniquely Beautiful

Through meticulous attention to detail, the geisha was an image of exquisite beauty. She created a world surrounding her beauty in which no other could replicate. Make yourself uniquely beautiful. Tend to your beauty, personalizing it with extra touches so that you create an aura that a man longs to be near.

Ritual 2 Embrace Your Femininity

Your feminine mystique is your natural gift and strength as a woman. Accentuate and allow it to be present in all of you – from how your sleeve slips past your wrist, revealing the softness of your skin and smooth line of your arm, to how your feminine scent floats from your neck past your lovely hair. You possess what a man desires to see and feel in a woman. Your feminine presence alone will draw him to you. A woman's feminine attributes have been painted and sculpted by artists for centuries. Your feminine being is a work of art that is admired and valued by men.

Ritual 3 Demonstrate Subtle Sex Appeal

When you reveal just enough to tempt a man to imagine, the more intrigued he will be. As you possess subtle sexiness, you will tease a man with your presence and the silhouette of your figure. When you walk into a room, the image of you will turn a man's head. It is an image that he will never forget as the woman he desires.

Ritual 4 Embody Elegance

An elegant woman is understated, yet is noticed by all in her presence as she stands out among all others. To possess elegance is to exuberate beauty in every movement. As the geisha was elegant in the way she wore her kimono and performed a dance piece and played a musical instrument, you will exemplify grace with every movement. Your goal will never be to draw attention to yourself, but the attention will be granted as men admire the beauty that you resonate – a beauty that is exquisite and regal.

Ritual 5 Exhibit Intelligence and Accomplishment

If you have little to stimulate a man beyond your looks, then you cannot excite a man to fully desire you over time. You must understand that as time passes, you should further develop your art and become more interesting and accomplished as a means of bettering yourself. Your ability to entice a man with your intelligence and wit is more powerful than and as sexy as your physical beauty.

Ritual 6 Exercise Humility in Everything You Do

Possessing humility will make every part of your being more beautiful. Behind the geisha's exquisite beauty and vast accomplishments lays humility, leaving her imprint on history as the image of a man's ideal beauty. When you are humble about your achievements, you exhibit maturity and wisdom. You understand that the value in an act lies with your appreciation, not what you gain over others in the end. By being humble, every single one of your actions and successes, regardless of the magnitude, is more beautiful because it does not seek recognition.

Ritual 7 Act with Kindness

To act with kindness is to create harmony in a relationship. Harmony was prized above any other social value in the flower and willow world as it led to meaningful, long-lasting relationships. When you speak and act from a genuinely kind place, the world you create is a retreat where a man longs to be. You become the place where a man knows that there is never criticism or confrontation and where he is sure to enjoy his time. Your kind demeanor is what a man always wants to know and feel.

Ritual 8 Perform Thoughtful Acts

To be thoughtful is to exhibit depth. It shows that you are conscious and caring and that it is important to you to go out of your way for those who are close to you. The geisha's thoughtfulness led to building strong bonds with her guests. Exhibiting thoughtfulness is an essential element in creating a strong bond with a man. When you perform a personalized thoughtful act, a man will feel a unique connection to you. Your thoughtful acts extend beyond showing that you care. They are what will make your friendships and relationships last a lifetime.

Ritual 9 Be the Prize that is Pursued

As the geisha and flower and willow world were mysterious and alluring, there should be exclusiveness about you as well. A man is attracted to the mystery in a woman. There are many aspects and layers that make up your being. Reveal them slowly.

Ritual 10 Wait to Give Yourself to a Man

Your intimacy should not be easily given. By not giving up your exclusivity, you are more desirable to many men with each hoping he is the worthy one. There will be many who hope to be intimate with you. Remain a dream in their imagination. For the man who is worthy, he will forever desire what is solely his.

Ritual 11 Be at Ease in All of Your Endeavors

Men sought out the flower and willow world because of the calm and peacefulness that the geisha offered. She was light in her presence and at ease in even the most stressful situations. To be with you should be a retreat for a man. He will feel as if he is entering a world that is inviting whenever he is near you. A man will feel your calmness and feel secure. It is your light attitude and ability to easily laugh that will draw him to you, resulting in him missing you when you are away.

Ritual 12 Show Your Appreciation

To let a man know that you appreciate him is to make him feel valued. A simple thank you or a few words of appreciation will make him feel good and he will continue to give himself to you. As he gives to you and you demonstrate that you appreciate him, you will connect further with one another and he will continue to possess a natural fondness for you.

Ritual 13 Be Compassionate

By possessing the ability to exhibit compassion, you are showing emotional strength as you are able to open your heart and feel for another. This requires great awareness and sensitivity. The geisha was compassionate and able to feel in a way most others could not. The ability to possess true awareness and express compassion are two of the greatest skills that you can master. By mastering these two skills you will create a higher and rare emotional bond with a man.

Ritual 14 Be Deliberate in Your Communication

Communicating well is a key essential to success in all relationships. It is especially important with a man since there are many emotions that the two of you will feel as you spend more time together. The way in which you express your deepest feelings to one another is crucial to building and sustaining the relationship. If you are thoughtful and deliberate with your communication, then you will reduce stress and conflict. A man will feel a strong connection to you when it is easy to communicate and be with you. Being able to communicate well will bring you success in all aspects of your life, particularly with a man.

Ritual 15 Be Attentive at Key Moments

Your attentiveness will create a bond with a man for which he will seek throughout his life. When you are attentive to a man at the times that it is most important, you are fully present and giving your best during those moments. Your focus is on the journey of the act itself, rather than what will be gained in the end. By giving during the moment, you will experience a special connection with a man. The strong relationship that you develop over time will exist as a result of your awareness of the key moments that have been occurring in the present.

Ritual 16 Deeply Connect to a Man

To deeply connect to a man is to be caring and non-judgmental, while asking the right questions at the right moments. It is about being able to eliminate any selfishness in order to help a man, while being yourself so that you are able to remain a strong and independent woman. It takes a very special woman to serve as a facilitator who helps a man better understand himself. The geisha knew how to make a man feel comfortable enough to open up his deepest feelings to her. She was a trusted confidante and close friend. When you establish a deep connection with a man, you have created an irreplaceable bond that will help him navigate his journey through life.

Ritual 17 Allow a Man to Embrace His Maleness

To be a geisha meant to be a woman who is like no other. At the heart of the geisha was the intent of being the ideal female partner for a man. As you become the best woman that you can be, understand that a man desires to be the best man that he can be. There are qualities that he must embody to achieve his goals. The same holds true for you. Embrace his desire to be a leader, provider, and protector. It is the balance between the male and female partnership that will help maintain your strong relationship.

Ritual 18 Be an Independent Woman

To be an independent woman is to have ideas and opinions that are uniquely yours and to understand how to achieve success. It means that you must stay genuine and not put on a false identity in a relationship. You understand that a man admires your independence as he loves you for who you are. A man will want to be with you because you stand out among all others.

Ritual 19 Be a Dynamic Hostess

The geisha exhibited her superior skills and qualities by being a dynamic hostess to her guests. Guests sought her out because all that she provided could not be replicated elsewhere. By embodying all of *The Rituals*, you will be the ideal female companion and will naturally be an excellent hostess. Your presence and what you offer will showcase your inner and outer beauty, as well as your vast accomplishments and intelligence. You will possess the gift of lifting spirits and making people happy. You will be the ultimate companion desired by many. A man will long to be the one who you solely love.

Ritual 20 Keep a Man Intrigued for a Lifetime

The geisha has been described as a butterfly – light, colorful, beautiful and delicate – fluttering into the night and out, leaving as exquisitely as she entered. Be uniquely memorable, leaving an impression on a man that he forever wants to experience again and again.

How *The Rituals* changed Dawn's life

Before *The Geisha Secret* was published, Dawn asked if she could read it because she was searching for an answer as to why she was still single in her late thirties. Her situation did not make sense to her. She had been raised in a close-knit family who nurtured and encouraged her to succeed. She attended an Ivy League college, went to work for a start-up company after graduation, and made more money than most people hoped to make in a lifetime. Dawn was not only smart and accomplished, but also beautiful. She worked hard every day at making herself beautiful – practicing yoga and pilates, and frequenting spas for facials and other body treatments. The only reasonable answer that Dawn could come up with as to why she was single was that she was having horrible luck with men.

In search of clarity, Dawn eagerly took *The Geisha Secret* and said she would get back right away with her thoughts. A month passed with no word from her. When she finally did reach out, she was not very enthusiastic. She confirmed that she had read it. She politely remarked, "Thank you," in a tone that sounded more like, "No thanks." Dawn was silent again until she re-emerged weeks later. This time, she responded saying that she had read *The Geisha Secret* on the first day that she received it, but it took her some time to really respond because she had to digest it. Would following the ways of the geisha really make a difference? Dawn decided that she had nothing to lose if she followed all of *The Rituals* and committed to live by the practices of the geisha.

At first, it was harder than Dawn imagined. After a great date, she wanted to call her date immediately and tell him how much fun she had. Instead, she found activities to distract herself and counted on friends to stop her from picking up the phone. This was part of Dawn's issue. She was overeager and made it too easy for men to gain all of her attention. If a man she liked did not give her ample warning and asked her to meet him in an hour for a date, then she would do it. Dawn believed that by always being available, men would like her more. In turn, she showed how much she cared by doing exactly what they wanted. Unfortunately, how men perceived Dawn was different from how Dawn perceived herself. Men viewed Dawn as pretty, smart, and nice, *but* always available and too aggressive in her pursuit. In other words, Dawn was an acceptable girl to call when no one else was available. She was never the woman who intrigued men or was passionately desired, despite her physical beauty and vast accomplishments.

Although Dawn was already practicing some of the aspects of *The Rituals* when she first read *The Geisha Secret,* it did not matter because she lost her allure from the onset and diminished her great qualities. Men thought that she could be very pretty, but her eagerness to impress a man by acting masculine made her unsexy. The answer to Dawn's dating problems was that she had to be committed to all of *The Rituals* and practice them in one unified way. Determined and having tried all other methods to solve her dating dilemma, Dawn stopped calling her dates a few hours after she saw them. She also waited for them to ask her out again and eliminated mentioning her future plans to marry and have a family. She allowed men to lead the conversations rather than dominate so that she could prove she was strong and intelligent. She let men pursue her and what she quickly discovered was that they were asking her out for second, third, fourth, and fifth dates. For the first time in her life, Dawn sat back and did not try to push relationships forward.

Amongst the men she dated, Dawn started seeing Nick. Dawn thought and hoped Nick might be *the one,* and she desperately wanted to tell him so. She even reached out to friends asking over and over if it was ok to call. She knew the answer was no. When Nick, unprompted, started calling Dawn every day, she realized she had made the right decision. Within a short time, he started referring to Dawn as his girlfriend, which was what Dawn wanted. It had finally happened – an amazing man was passionately in love with her. Months went by and Dawn and Nick became more serious. They traveled across the world together, shared dinners with their close friends, met each other's families, and spent holidays with them. It was as if Dawn and Nick had been dating for years. Then Dawn got what she most desired in the world – a marriage proposal from a man she loved.

Dawn's life was forever changed because she had embraced and embodied all of *The Rituals.* Just as incredible was that Nick was not able to find a woman that satisfied him until he met Dawn. Nick wanted an ideal female companion, but it took him a longtime to find her. If you practice and exemplify all of the traits of *The Rituals,* then you can become the ideal woman. If you continue to incorporate the ways of the geisha well into your relationship, then you will always be desired. Today Dawn and Nick are married. Dawn still refers back to *The Rituals* because they help to sustain a harmonious marriage.

Keep a man intrigued – practice *Ritual 20.*

As you embody *The Rituals* and they become a natural extension of who you are, you will become the woman men desire. You will intrigue men because you are the woman who they have imagined in their dreams, but have rarely met in the flesh. A woman who follows *The Geisha Secret* is a woman who men notice. They watch her as she confidently moves while humbly entering a room. She touches every man in her presence with her beauty and kindness. She moves gracefully and she listens attentively to others. When she speaks, her wit charms and her feminine voice dances across the room, filling the minds of the men around her. She is the woman men want to have forever.

Each geisha is like a flower, beautiful in her own way, and like a willow tree, gracious, flexible and strong. [5]

www.thegeishasecret.com

Glossary

asobi: play

atotori: a geiko who is an heir to an okiya and its successor. She carries the last name of the okiya through birth or adoption and lives in the okiya throughout her career or life. [1]

danna: a geisha's patron

erikae ceremony: the formal ceremony when a senior maiko graduates to a geiko

flower and willow world: the geisha society as a whole [2]

geiko: a full-fledged geisha (specifically in Kyoto). Geiko translates to woman of art.

genkan: the traditional Japanese entranceway of a home

geta clogs: shoes worn by geiko

Gion Kobu: a district of Kyoto and the most famous and traditional karyukai [3]

hanamachi: a geisha district within the flower and willow world. Also known as flower towns.

hikizuri: the kimono worn by a maiko. Unlike an ordinary kimono, it has long sleeves and a wide train, and is worn slung low on the back of the neck. [4]

iki: a very special Japanese aesthetic that refers to a highly cultivated but not solemn sensibility, as open to broad jokes and puns as it is deeply versed in traditional high arts. Ultra-aesthetic, but playful and witty. [5]

jikata: a geisha specializing in playing music and singing [6] *kaburenjo*: dance and music school dedicated to the training of geisha.

karyukai: special districts in Japan dedicated to the enjoyment of aesthetic pleasure and where the professionally trained female artists known as geisha live and work. Karyukai is also known as the flower and willow world. [7]

maiko: an apprentice geisha (specifically in Kyoto). Maiko translates to woman of dance.

maioghi: a special fan geiko and maiko use when dancing

minarai: an apprentice maiko

minarai-jaya: a single ochaya where a minarai's initial training is primarily spent

Mother: the owner of an ochaya

natori: the highest form of art

Nihon Buyo: a traditional and refined dance that is an art form intended for entertainment on stage

nochiseki: the final part of the Japanese tea ceremony

Noh: a classical Japanese musical drama that has been performed since the 14th century

obi: a broad sash tied around the kimono

ochaya: very exclusive banquet facilities where maiko and geiko perform and entertain at private parties for select groups of invited patrons. Ochaya translates to teahouses. [8]

okiya: a house where maiko and geiko live

okobo clogs: platform clogs worn by maiko

Onesan: a maiko's Older Sister, carefully chosen to serve as her role model and mentor

ozashiki: an intimate, private party where geisha entertain guests in an ochaya

roji: the garden through which one passes to enter the Japanese tea ceremony

ryubi: willow brows. The geisha's eyebrows are sculpted in the *ryubi* style to create the ideal shape.

san-san-kudo: the ceremony turning a minarai into a maiko and formally binding her to an Older Sister. San-san-kudo translates to three-three-nine, taking of an oath nine times. [9]

shakuhachi: a Japanese bamboo flute

shamisen: a three-stringed Japanese musical instrument played with a plectrum called a bachi

shikomi: the first apprentice of an aspiring geisha before becoming a minarai (watching apprentice). Shikomi translates to maid.

shironuri: the white mask painted on a geisha's face

tachikata: a geisha specializing in dance [10]

tamagushi: term used in the Kyoto geisha district Asakusa to calculate units of time or flower charge for an ozashiki. Tamagushi translates to an offering of a sacred spring to a Shinto God.

tan: cloth

tatami room: a traditional, Japanese style room where geisha usually entertain *tokonoma*: an alcove in the wall for the display of decorative scrolls, flower arrangements, bonsai plants or decorative objects

tsukubai: stone water basin in a tea garden used for ritual washing of the hands

wajutsu: the art of trivial conversation [11]

wareshinobu: the first hairstyle a maiko wears. The hair is swept up and sculpted into a mass on top of the head. It is secured by *kanoko* (red silk bands) and decorated with kanzashi (the stick pin ornaments distinctive of the geisha look). [12]

zori sandals: shoes worn by geiko

Notes

The Geisha Mystique

1. Lesley Downer, *Women of the Pleasure Quarters: The Secret History of the Geisha* (New York, NY: Broadway Books, 2002), p. 511.

2. Jodi Cobb, *Geisha: The Life, the Voices, the Art* (New York, NY: Knopf, 1998), p. 34.

The Rituals

1. Cobb, *Geisha: The Life, the Voices, the Art*, p. 5.

Ritual 1 Make Yourself Uniquely Beautiful

1. John Gallagher, *Geisha: A Unique World of Tradition, Elegance, and Art* (London: PRC Publishing Ltd, 2003), p. 212.

2. Mineko Iwasaki and Rande Brown, *Geisha: A Life* (New York, NY: Washington Square Press, 2003), p. 66.

3. Iwasaki and Brown, *Geisha: A Life*, p. 78.

4. Iwasaki and Brown, *Geisha: A Life*, p. 236.

5. Iwasaki and Brown, *Geisha: A Life*, p. 140.

Ritual 2 Embrace Your Femininity

1. Gallagher, *Geisha: A Unique World of Tradition, Elegance, and Art*, p. 140.

2. Gallagher, *Geisha: A Unique World of Tradition, Elegance, and Art*, p. 146.

3. Iwasaki and Brown, *Geisha: A Life*, p. 140.

4. Downer, *Women of the Pleasure Quarters: The Secret History of the Geisha*, p. 9.

Ritual 3 Have Subtle Sex Appeal

1. Gallagher, *Geisha: A Unique World of Tradition, Elegance, and Art*, p. 18.

2. Michelle Green, "Amazing Grace: The Art and Ordeal of the Kimono," *The New York Times*, March 2, 2008, online.

3. Green, "Amazing Grace: The Art and Ordeal of the Kimono".

4. Cobb, *Geisha: The Life, the Voices, the Art*, p. 11.

Ritual 4 Embody Elegance

1. Gallagher, *Geisha: A Unique World of Tradition, Elegance, and Art*, p. 150-151.

2. Gallagher, *Geisha: A Unique World of Tradition, Elegance, and Art*, p. 93.

3. David McNeill, "Turning Japanese: the first foreign geisha," *The Independent UK*, January 24, 2008, online.

4. Komomo, *A Geisha's Journey: My Life As a Kyoto Apprentice* (Tokyo: Kodansha International, 2008), p. 9.

5. Green, "Amazing Grace: The Art and Ordeal of the Kimono".

6. Downer, *Women of the Pleasure Quarters: The Secret History of the Geisha*, p. 83.

7. Gallagher, *Geisha: A Unique World of Tradition, Elegance, and Art*, p. 31.

Ritual 5 Exhibit Intelligence and Accomplishment

1. Gallagher, *Geisha: A Unique World of Tradition, Elegance, and Art*, p. 86.

2. Gallagher, *Geisha: A Unique World of Tradition, Elegance, and Art*, p. 154.

3. Gallagher, *Geisha: A Unique World of Tradition, Elegance, and Art*, p. 158.

4. Downer, *Women of the Pleasure Quarters: The Secret History of the Geisha*, p. 6.

5. Gallagher, *Geisha: A Unique World of Tradition, Elegance, and Art*, p. 159.

6. Komomo, *A Geisha's Journey: My Life As a Kyoto Apprentice*, p. 14.

7. Gallagher, *Geisha: A Unique World of Tradition, Elegance, and Art*, p. 8.

Ritual 6 Exercise Humility in Everything You Do

1. Gallagher, *Geisha: A Unique World of Tradition, Elegance, and Art*, p. 35.

2. McNeill, "Turning Japanese: the first foreign geisha".

3. Iwasaki and Brown, *Geisha: A Life*, p. 84.

4. Gallagher, *Geisha: A Unique World of Tradition, Elegance, and Art*, p. 178.
5. Iwasaki and Brown, *Geisha: A Life*, p. 59.
6. Elaine Lies, "Globe-trotting geisha shares secrets in new book," *Reuters*, April 22, 2008, online.

Ritual 7 Act with Kindness

1. Iwasaki and Brown, *Geisha: A Life*, p. 137.
2. Iwasaki and Brown, *Geisha: A Life*, p. 137.
3. Iwasaki and Brown, *Geisha: A Life*, p. 5.

Ritual 8 Perform Thoughtful Acts

1. Komomo, *A Geisha's Journey: My Life As a Kyoto Apprentice*, p. 60.
2. Iwasaki and Brown, *Geisha: A Life*, p. 170.
3. Iwasaki and Brown, *Geisha: A Life*, p. 5.

Ritual 9 Be the Prize That Is Pursued

1. Gallagher, *Geisha: A Unique World of Tradition, Elegance, and Art*, p. 200.
2. Ward, "Butterflies of the Evening".
3. Gallagher, *Geisha: A Unique World of Tradition, Elegance, and Art*, p. 198.
4. Ward, "Butterflies of the Evening".

Ritual 10 Wait to Give Yourself to a Man

1. Iwasaki and Brown, *Geisha: A Life*, p. 78.
2. Cobb, *Geisha: The Life, the Voices, the Art*, p. 5.
3. Gallagher, *Geisha: A Unique World of Tradition, Elegance, and Art*, p. 118.
4. Gallagher, *Geisha: A Unique World of Tradition, Elegance, and Art*, p. 26.

Ritual 11 Be at Ease in All Your Endeavors

1. Komomo, *A Geisha's Journey: My Life As a Kyoto Apprentice*, p. 8.
2. Iwasaki and Brown, *Geisha: A Life*, p. 41.

3. Iwasaki and Brown, *Geisha: A Life,* p. 60.

4. Iwasaki and Brown, *Geisha: A Life,* p. 60.

5. Iwasaki and Brown, *Geisha: A Life,* p. 5.

Ritual 12 Show Your Appreciation

1. Iwasaki and Brown, *Geisha: A Life,* p. 78.

2. Iwasaki and Brown, *Geisha: A Life,* p. 78-79.

3. Gallagher, *Geisha: A Unique World of Tradition, Elegance, and Art,* p. 83.

Ritual 13 Be Compassionate

1. Cobb, *Geisha: The Life, the Voices, the Art,* p. 34.

2. Komomo, *A Geisha's Journey: My Life As a Kyoto Apprentice,* p. 8.

Ritual 14 Be Deliberate in Your Communication

1. Iwasaki and Brown, *Geisha: A Life,* p. 104.

2. Iwasaki and Brown, *Geisha: A Life,* p. 104.

3. Iwasaki and Brown, *Geisha: A Life,* p. 179.

Ritual 15 Be Attentive at Key Moments

1. Ward, "Butterflies of the Evening".

Ritual 16 Deeply Connect to a Man

1. Iwasaki and Brown, *Geisha: A Life,* p. 79.

2. Iwasaki and Brown, *Geisha: A Life,* p. 194-195.

3. Iwasaki and Brown, *Geisha: A Life,* p. 135.

4. Iwasaki and Brown, *Geisha: A Life,* p. 170.

Ritual 17 Allow a Man to Embrace His Maleness

1. Cobb, *Geisha: The Life, the Voices, the Art,* p. 5 & 14.

2. Iwasaki and Brown, *Geisha: A Life*, p. 51.

3. Cobb, *Geisha: The Life, the Voices, the Art*, p. 8.

Ritual 18 Be an Independent Woman

1. Gallagher, *Geisha: A Unique World of Tradition, Elegance, and Art*, p. 31.

2. Iwasaki and Brown, *Geisha: A Life*, p. 188.

3. Iwasaki and Brown, *Geisha: A Life*, p. 3.

4. Cobb, *Geisha: The Life, the Voices, the Art*, p. 8.

Ritual 19 Be a Dynamic Hostess

1. Iwasaki and Brown, *Geisha: A Life*, p. 135-136.

2. Gallagher, *Geisha: A Unique World of Tradition, Elegance, and Art*, p. 183.

3. Iwasaki and Brown, *Geisha: A Life*, p. 135-139.

4. Cobb, *Geisha: The Life, the Voices, the Art*, p. 7.

5. Cobb, *Geisha: The Life, the Voices, the Art*, p. 7.

6. Gallagher, *Geisha: A Unique World of Tradition, Elegance, and Art*, p. 15.

7. Iwasaki and Brown, *Geisha: A Life*, p. 194.

8. Gallagher, *Geisha: A Unique World of Tradition, Elegance, and Art*, p. 8 & 16.

Ritual 20 Keep a Man Intrigued

1. Cobb, *Geisha: The Life, the Voices, the Art*, p. 5.

2. Miki Tanikawa, "In Kyoto, a Call to Not Trample the Geisha," *The New York Times*, April 7, 2009 online.

3. Gallagher, *Geisha: A Unique World of Tradition, Elegance, and Art*, p. 8.

4. Iwasaki and Brown, *Geisha: A Life*, p. 1.

5. Gallagher, *Geisha: A Unique World of Tradition, Elegance, and Art*, p. 89.

Glossary

1. Iwasaki and Brown, *Geisha: A Life*, p. 3.

2. Gallagher, *Geisha: A Unique World of Tradition, Elegance, and Art*, p. 255.

3. Iwasaki and Brown, *Geisha: A Life*, p. 2.

4. Iwasaki and Brown, *Geisha: A Life*, p. 141.

5. Gallagher, *Geisha: A Unique World of Tradition, Elegance, and Art*, p. 8.

6. Gallagher, *Geisha: A Unique World of Tradition, Elegance, and Art*, p. 255.

7. Iwasaki and Brown, *Geisha: A Life*, p. 1.

8. Iwasaki and Brown, *Geisha: A Life*, p. 3.

9. Gallagher, *Geisha: A Unique World of Tradition, Elegance, and Art*, p. 149.

10. Gallagher, *Geisha: A Unique World of Tradition, Elegance, and Art*, p. 255.

11. Gallagher, *Geisha: A Unique World of Tradition, Elegance, and Art*, p. 89.

12. Iwasaki and Brown, *Geisha: A Life*, p. 140.

Made in the USA
Middletown, DE
15 July 2021